Even Coarser Sport

MICHAEL GREEN

Even Coarser Sport

Illustrated by JOHN JENSEN

HUTCHINSON OF LONDON

Hutchinson & Co. (Publishers) Ltd
3 Fitzroy Square, London W1P 6JD

London Melbourne Sydney Auckland
Wellington Johannesburg and agencies
throughout the world

First published 1978

Set in VIP Baskerville by Input Typesetting Ltd

Printed in Great Britain by The Anchor Press Ltd
and bound by Wm Brendon & Son Ltd,
both of Tiptree, Essex

British Library Cataloguing in Publication data

Green, Michael
    Even coarser sport.
    1. Sports – Anecdotes, facetiae, satire etc
    2. Games – Anecdotes, facetiae, satire etc
    I. Title
    796'.02'07   GV707

ISBN 0 09 136130 3

Contents

	Foreword	7
1	When Fun is a Dirty Word	9
2	The Horrors of Being a Professional Coarse Sportsman	12
3	Nation shall Scrum Down with Nation	17
4	A Tour round Sport's Gin, Tonic and Crisps Circuit	21
5	Box and Cox	26
6	Max Boyce's Cousin	29
7	Trouble up the Creek	32
8	An Appeal from the Golf Coarse	36
9	Squire Haggard in the Field	40
10	When Truth is Funnier than Fiction	44
11	Disco Train's Maiden Journey	50
12	Turn NSW, Avoid Prams	53
13	Woe to the Uncircumcised Batsman	57
14	The Curse of the Poison Dwarf	59
15	Some Coarse Customers	62
16	When the Wheezes Won't Work	68
17	The Sound of the Master's Name	72
18	Bedroom Secret Turns Rabbit into Tiger	75
19	At Last – I've Got Golf Taped	78
20	The Great Grub Street Stakes	82
21	A Trip down Memory Drain	87
22	Games People Play with Olympics	94
23	The Art of Coarse Rowing	98
24	An Ode on the Battle of Twickenham	102
25	The Day Their Dreams Came True	105

26	The Buy, Buy Blues	108
27	Sponsored Nightmare	113
28	The Coarse Acting Show	116
29	Things that will Never Change in Sport	121
30	Fiona's Honeymoon Night	126

Foreword

Some of the material in this book is new and some has been reproduced, with or without adaptation, from articles and broadcasts. The following chapters are based on articles by me which originally appeared in the *Sunday Times*: 'A Tour round Sport's Gin, Tonic and Crisps Circuit', 'Disco Train's Maiden Journey', 'Turn NSW, Avoid Prams', 'When the Wheezes Won't Work', 'Bedroom Secret Turns Rabbit into Tiger', 'At Last – I've Got Golf Taped', 'The Great Grub Street Stakes', 'Games People Play with Olympics', 'The Art of Coarse Rowing', 'The Day Their Dreams Came True', 'Sponsored Nightmare' and 'Things That Will Never Change in Sport'.

Other acknowledgements are: to *Punch* for 'The Horrors of Being a Professional Coarse Sportsman', to *Radio Times* for 'Nation shall Scrum Down with Nation' and 'An Appeal from the Golf Course', to the BBC for 'Box and Cox', 'Woe to the Uncircumcised Batsman' and 'The Curse of the Poisoned Dwarf', to *Yachting Monthly* for 'Trouble up the Creek', and to *Whitbread Way* for 'Some Coarse Customers'.

The last chapter, 'Fiona's Honeymoon Night', is reprinted from *Michael Green's Rugby Alphabet* (Pelham Books). This is now out of print, and as many readers of her earlier adventures have asked about Fiona's fate, I thought I owed it to them to reproduce the story of her last fling.

MICHAEL GREEN

1 When Fun is a Dirty Word

In *The Art of Coarse Sport* I define a Coarse Sportsman as 'one, who, when his club receives a grant from the National Playing Fields Association, wants to spend it on extending the bar'. There are, of course, definitions for individual sports, such as that for a Coarse Sailor, 'One who in a crisis forgets nautical language and shouts, "For God's sake, turn left" '; or Coarse Rugby, 'A game played by fewer than 15-a-side, most of whom should be totally unfit'. This book is a collection of the further experiences and thoughts of a Coarse Sportsman, some new, others from my broadcasts or articles. In presenting it, I make no apology for saying that today as never before the world needs people who are Coarse Sportsmen or Sportswomen. When sport is played for money, national prestige, career improvement, fame, self-aggrandisement, commercial reasons, advertising reasons, medical reasons, psychiatric reasons and political reasons, in fact for every reason except FUN, it's more important than ever to maintain islands of sanity, beery cricket matches on filthy pastures, rum-sodden rugby games on Sunday afternoons, soccer on the park before the pubs open.

Not that your average Coarse Sportsman is aware he is playing a part in sport's destiny. His lot is much more likely to be abuse from all and sundry, especially the ruling bodies of various sports and Government bureaucrats, all of whom regard him as a menace to their neat, tailored structure, because they like everyone to be organized, preferably in enormous sport complexes where men in track suits can keep an eye on everyone and make sure they're not enjoying themselves too much. Coarse Sportsmen are also regarded as a menace by many clubs, whose ambitions to progress ever upward are not helped by a fifth team composed of incompetents and cowards.

One reason why Coarse Sport is so important today is because leisure has suddenly become work. I suppose it's the great paradox of our times, that whereas all of us have much more free time than people did in the past, when the hours of work were longer and holidays shorter, leisure is taking on all the qualities of earning a living. It's becoming over-organized, compulsive, compulsory and competitive. Just look at the way rugby and club cricket sides have embraced the league principle and the virtual extinction of good-class amateur soccer. Even village cricket is in leagues these days.

I went into a rugby pavilion recently and the coach had installed a blackboard there on which was written the text for that evening's instruction – namely:

THINK! SCAN SITUATION! BALL WANTED! SECOND-PHASE POSSESSION VITAL! COMMIT OPPOSITION!

All very necessary, no doubt, in the frenetic world of modern sport but I couldn't help thinking it seemed a long way in spirit from the field near the canal at Greenford, Middlesex, where our skipper was asked by an opposing captain before a game, 'Would your side mind tackling our winger gently, as he has a steel plate in his skull?' But then, it is typical of coarse rugby that the casualties, the sick, the lame, the halt and the aged go on the wings, so in any match the touchlines are patrolled by players looking like something out of Napoleon's retreat from Moscow. There is, of course, no question of them running or tackling, they just sort of shamble up and down.

It's also a long way from the little local side in Gloucestershire a West Country relative used to take me to watch as a boy when I went visiting on holiday. They were always there whenever I went, so I asked my uncle why they didn't play away occasionally.

'They'm can't afford to play away,' he said. 'They can hardly afford to play at home.'

My childish mind was very impressed by this side. They

had a front row with only twenty five teeth between them. The hooker had a belly so large it trailed on the ground during the set scrums. His trousers were held up by an old pyjama string which dangled down, and opponents used to infuriate him by deliberately treading on it. The most unusual player, however, was the full-back, who was deaf and dumb and communicated by loud honking noises and strange gestures which struck terror into new opponents.

As for cricket, somehow I don't think today's club leagues would find room for the man who used to play in my team in the Midlands. He had an artificial leg which on one occasion disintegrated under a direct hit from a powerful drive and fell out of his trousers in a shower of bits and pieces.

Even in park soccer, players have started jumping around like maniacs when they score, and kissing and cuddling each other like any league team. When *I* played soccer on Sunday mornings anyone who scored had to buy a round of drinks, but I suppose that's all gone now as well.

I think the word 'hard work' sums up much modern leisure. Fortunately Coarse Sport is not completely dead. Bald-headed men can still be seen wandering aimlessly around football pitches of both codes; living skeletons may be noticed flaying tennis balls wildly in all directions on public courts (they wouldn't be allowed to join a tennis club, of course), and only the other day I actually saw someone *laugh* on a posh golf course in Surrey. Mind you, I think it was because his opponent had just sliced a ball into someone's greenhouse. Golfers in general only laugh at other people's mistakes, not their own, but it does show a glimmering of the true spirit.

Perhaps one day the reaction will set in and some youngster of the next century will pick up a tennis racquet or a golf club or a rugby ball and say, 'Hey dad, playing with this ought to be *fun*.' Alas, his father will probably reply, 'Don't ever mention that filthy word again in this house.'

I dedicated *The Art of Coarse Sport* to 'Those who are not much good'. I dedicate this volume to those who are even worse. Let us hope the future is in their hands, even if the ball isn't.

2 The Horrors of Being a Professional Coarse Sportsman

The trouble with my sporting life is that I make a living by being bad at games. That is to say, I make money by writing allegedly funny books and articles about what it feels like to be a Coarse Sportsman, one who experiences the lower depths of inferiority and incompetence.

This makes me a sort of professional at being an amateur, which is a rather difficult position. It's certainly had a disastrous effect on my own enjoyment of sport, since no one is prepared to divorce me from my books. As always with the comedian, no one really believes he can ever be serious.

It's quite true that in one book I describe being sent off a rugby field for smoking, or rather not so much for smoking as for asking the referee for a light. But it may come as a surprise to those who have read that to learn that I don't consider myself too bad at most games. I played rugby until I was thirty-three and if it is true that I latterly played mostly for Ealing B it is also true that I once had a trial for Leicester.

Yet following publication of *The Art of Coarse Rugby* I was pretty well driven from the game by the attitude of fellow players who insisted on regarding everything I did as screamingly funny. Hoots of laughter would greet a magnificent penalty goal; howls of mirth hailed a sensational try; even if I crashed someone to the ground with a bone-shaking tackle he would say, 'That was the funniest thing that's happened to me for years,' as they carried him off.

Mercifully my rugby career would have come to an end soon, anyway, but this unenviable reputation has followed me into other sports.

Take golf, for instance. Apart from a tendency to burst into tears on missing a putt I was reasonably happy and competent until I wrote *The Art of Coarse Golf*, which the local paper described as 'a beezer, rib-tickling snort for children from eight to eighty'. (*The Times Literary Supplement* was less enthusiastic. It said something like, 'Mr Green's modest volume may raise an occasional faint smile.')

Faint smile or not, ever since I can't even walk on the first tee without people who know me falling about with hysterical laughter, nudging each other and cowering in mock terror as I swing. It's no good – Nicklaus himself couldn't drive decently when someone six feet away has actually fallen on his knees and is reciting the first line of the Lord's Prayer. To make it worse, half of them haven't even read the blasted book – they've just heard that this geezer is some sort of literary comedian. It's no wonder that at my last golf-society meeting I succeeded in landing an approach shot in an ice-cream van on the A40.

One of the worse aspects of this crazy situation is that everyone I am playing becomes obsessed with the idea that *they*'ve got to play the clown. Cricketers drop catches off my bowling and then shout, 'That's a bit of Coarse fielding for you'; golfers who partner me lose the match with a slice into the next parish, and instead of apologizing become convulsed with mirth and bellow, 'There's another chapter for your next book.'

Actually, most people have a very unfunny idea of what is amusing. I am also becoming rather tired of the idea that if you happen to write you spend your whole life searching for material, no matter what the cost. Recently I was complaining bitterly to a friend about our old cricket captain, one of those fussy little self-important dictators who persistently batted me number eleven no matter how many runs I made because I was once late for a game when my car broke down ('Completely irresponsible' was doubtless his description of me). 'Ah,' said my friend, 'but surely you were grateful for the chance to gather *such wonderful material*.' Although that experience is mild compared with what happened when I was lying in hospital in some discomfort and a drivelling visitor told me, 'Still, I suppose it all makes you a better writer.' If I hadn't been in plaster up to my waist I would have hit him.

It could be said it's all my own fault for writing exaggerated books about how incompetent idiots behave at sport. After all, if one persistently recalls vomiting at half-time when playing for the Extra B, people are inclined to doubt your sporting prowess. I, however, am firmly of the opinion that my books are hardly exaggerated at all. Experience shows that no writer can ever invent anything as funny as what actually happens in life.

Conversely, many so-called 'serious' sports writers deal largely in fantasies, a dream world of phoney crises, dramas, and lies. What other word but fantasy can be used when rich young footballers who quarrel with their managers are described as being 'crucified'? It's not my fault if I played for years with a rugby team where the wing three-quarter used to leave the field for a rest every time he scored, and once actually went and played for a team on the next pitch who were one short. ('They were a much better crowd than you lot,' he said on his return). It was true.

During a television programme, I asked the interviewer, who was casting doubts on my veracity, to choose what he considered to be the biggest lie in my books. He picked a yachting story in which the Calor gas leaked and, being heavier than air, collected in the bilges, from which it was bailed out in buckets, two men solemnly scooping nothing out of the bottom of the boat and pouring it into the water for hours. The story was, in fact, absolutely authentic.

A further drawback to being a professional incompetent is that not only are you supposed to be permanently in a fit of risible hysteria, but you are also presumed to be impervious to all insults. Recently an official of a sailing club asked if I would agree to open a new extension to the changing-rooms ('As you're such a well-known figure, ha, ha, ha'). Although feeling flattered, I suggested someone more famous would be better, perhaps Sir Alec Rose, who was a local man.

'Alec Rose?' came the reply. 'You can't ask a person like *him* to open a row of new lavatories.'

Letraset Limited
17/19 Valentine Place
Webber Street
London SE1

This, your Letraset catalogue, has been designed to make it easier for you to select, order, and use those products in our range which are relevant to your requirements. It has always been Letraset's policy to keep you, our ultimate customer informed of new developments, and at the same time take into account your needs and requirements when making additions to our range of products.

It would help us therefore if you could give us a few minutes of your time, and complete this short questionnaire.

Would you like to be placed on our mailing list?
Yes/No

Name _____

Position in company _____

Studio/Drawing Office/Other (Please state)

_____

Company _____

Address _____

_____

Who is your regular Letraset stockist?

Do you have an end user stock? Yes/No

Please tick those products used regularly.
Letraset Instant Lettering ☐ Letragraphica ☐
Letrafilm ☐ Letracolor ☐ Dry Color ☐
Letratone ☐ Letramarker ☐ Instantex ☐
Art sheets ☐ Architectural Range ☐
Electronics Symbols ☐ Project-a-type ☐
Technical Art ☐ Letratapes ☐
Special sheets ☐ Special tapes ☐
Letrasign ☐ Letracote gloss ☐ 101 ☐
Letrafilm Solvent ☐ Spray Adhesive ☐

What is your approximate total annual purchase of Letraset products?

_____

_____

_____

_____

What products or services would you like to see added to our range?

Letraset

'*Syd Nicholas passed peacefully away in hospital this afternoon*'

It's off the field, however, that life is most difficult. There may be some excuse for the view that while you're playing a sport you ought to look as if you're enjoying yourself, but afterwards a man is entitled to his own mood. Alas, it is presumed I shall every time be a fount of jollity and wit and teller of every sporting joke ever invented, as well as being totally incapable of having any serious feelings, such as grief or pain, whatsoever.

I shall never forget a small rugby club dinner, at which it fell to my lot, as a club official, to announce the death of an old vice-president.

I stood up and asked for silence, a request which was greeted with shrieks of laughter. I said I had a serious announcement to make (*more merriment and a shower of bread rolls and sugar cubes*).

'No, no, really,' I protested, 'this is not funny' (*collapse of half-a-dozen people*). 'As we all know, poor old Syd Nicholas has been in ailing health for some time' (*shouts of 'Yes, the old bastard got syph in the Boer War'*). 'No, please, this really is no joking matter, gentlemen' (*a positive explosion of jollity*). 'I am being serious' (a voice: *'First time in your life, then'*). 'It is with deep regret that I have to tell you that Syd Nicholas passed peacefully away in hospital this afternoon' (*complete collapse in mirth of whole assembly, mingled with shouts of, 'That's the unfunniest joke I've ever heard,' and, 'When's the pay-off coming?'*).

Later, in the toilets, I overheard one guest saying to another, 'It was that chap Green's own fault. He ought to have known no one would take him seriously. It was absolutely disgraceful to make a speech like that.'

To which his companion replied, 'Still, what can you expect. He's probably only getting material for *The Art of Coarse Speaking*.'

3 *Nation shall Scrum Down with Nation*

One of the sadder features of modern life is that everything tends to become standardized. Looking at a tower block in Zurich, for instance, one could be in London, Paris or Berlin for all the architectural difference.

This is as true of sport as any other human activity. The days when British football teams could be identified by the fact that they wore longer shorts than anybody else, have vanished, as have the days when the British could also be picked out because they played better and more sportingly than the opposition.

Even in rugby the distinctions between nations are becoming blurred by modern training methods and intensive coaching. Yet national characteristics doggedly survive, off the field if not so much on it these days.

Nowhere is this more true than in France. It is true French teams are no longer the undisciplined, arguing, shambling and often inspired mob they used to be, but French rugby still retains its own individual flavour. To start with, their team selection has all the public drama and bitterness of a US presidential election, with frequently a mass sweeping-away of the former players. Public accusations are common. Where a defeat at rugby in England may possibly inspire a modest letter to *The Times* ('Dear Sir, I believe the failure of the England rugby side is due to lack of Cambridge men in the team. . . .'), in France it can spark off bitter passions. Few will forget the famous occasion some years ago when thousands of Frenchmen marched round the pitch before an international at Stade Colombes, shaking their fists at the committee seats, and waving banners inscribed DÉMISSION AUX SELECTION-

NEURS. I can't imagine it happening at Twickenham, although I sometimes wish it would.

In fact, French rugby selectors receive just about as much respect from the public as do French politicians, which isn't saying much. But then, it could only happen in France that they should celebrate their seventy-fifth anniversary with a match against a World XV when the French Rugby Union was, in fact, only fifty seven years old at the time. The programme contained the names of eight threequarters in the world team and twelve forwards, one with a question mark against his name. Only three of those named actually played.

The Irish are the great story-tellers of rugby, the bards of the game as it were. A positive stream of yarns used to emanate from or around Tony O'Reilly, the great Lions winger, who made history by turning out for Ireland at Twickenham in 1970 in an emergency, seven years after his retirement from international rugby. At breakfast on the morning of the game O'Reilly asked Tom Kiernan about the problems of marking his opposite number.

Kiernan looked sourly at O'Reilly's expanding waistline and said bitterly, 'Just stand still and let the b—— run round you.' At the banquet after the game there was more ragging of O'Reilly, Kiernan beginning his speech by congratulating O'Reilly 'on having played his last game for Ireland'.

O'Reilly got his own-back by alleging that the only line-out instructions he got were, 'OK, O'Reilly, let's have it the usual way – low and crooked.'

The Irish (naturally) bring religion into their rugby, and holy water has been known to have been sprinkled over their front row in the dressing-room before a match (religious differences are submerged for the day). O'Reilly tells of an Irish threequarter who described a Welsh wing forward as 'a very mean fella with the boot and elbow and distinctly anti-clerical when he got you on the ground'.

For the Welsh, of course, rugby is a religion. A hoary legend says that when Keith Jarrett scored 19 points for Wales in their 34-21 victory over England in 1967 he missed the last bus to Newport and was stranded at the bus depot. A bus driver, seeing who it was, got a conductor and started to take out a special for the hero of the game. An inspector came along and said sternly, 'What's going on here?'

'It's Keith Jarrett. We're taking him home.'

'Put that bus back immediately,' said the inspector. 'And get out a double-decker. He might want to smoke.'

One might like to compare this with the way a famous England international was treated some years back. His rail fare to London, in the days before decimalization, always came to £2 19*s* 11*d*. He used to round this up to £3 and every time the treasurer knocked off the odd penny, so in the end he wrote: 'Rail fare – £2 19*s* 11*d*. Toilet: 1*d*. Total – £3. ' This was accepted without question.

But now rugby is spreading strongly, way beyond the traditional five nations of the Home Championship and the old British Empire. It used to be believed that 'foreigners' didn't have the right temperament for a game of controlled violence like rugby. I remember asking my old schoolmaster why they didn't play rugby in Europe and getting a reply something like this: 'Because they do not have the right spirit, my boy. If you handed-off a Spaniard for instance, he would stick a knife into you. Also, they cannot grow grass like we can in this country, where we are favoured by the Gulf Stream. Therefore, the ground is too hard for rugby, which is also why they don't play cricket.'

In fact the temperament theory may be backfiring these days. Rugby is spreading rapidly in America but there have been complaints from teams in the USA about foul play by visiting British sides, which leads one to ask whether in twenty years' time an American child might ask, 'Gee, pop, why don't we play the English at rugger any more?' and the reply could be, 'Because, son, the British don't have the right temperament. If you handed-off a Limey he would probably knife you. Also their grounds are not suitable. They don't make artificial turf as good as we do, which is why they can't play baseball.'

The spread of rugby behind the Iron Curtain in recent years has been particularly fascinating. A year or two back I watched a Polish club side on tour playing against a club in Lancashire. I must admit to having had a sneaking hope that they would march on the field shouting, 'Socialist greetings to our anti-fascist comrades from Burnley, and death to the revisionist running dogs,' but they were distressingly like anybody else and they won by two points in a fast game, refereed by a positive local genius, who got over the language problem by communicating in grunts, signs, snarls and pidgin-English words such as 'footski-upski'. The Poles were, in fact, generally more English than the English (except that they handled the ball better), and their behaviour after the match was almost a parody of how the beer-swilling English are supposed to behave. Within an hour they were drinking vast jugs of bitter and contributing to what they called the 'zinc-zonc' with strange Polish dirges, which I can only presume were the Eastern European equivalent of *Eskimo Nell*.

With Romania forging ahead to the state where she has recorded wins over France of all people, perhaps the balance of world rugby power is going to shift East. Romania has, of course, been a long time on the rugby scene, and it was in Bucharest during a Harlequins tour in the fifties that a Quins official is supposed to have tried to impress his hosts by beginning a speech with the Romanian words for 'Ladies and Gentlemen', which he carefully copied from a public lavatory. His little effort however, was greeted with grim silence. When he asked the interpreter what went wrong, the interpreter explained he had actually begun his speech by saying the Romanian for 'water closets and urinals'.

4 *A tour round Sport's Gin, Tonic and Crisps Circuit*

Probably the people who have benefited most from sponsorship in sport are the manufacturers of gin. These days it seems
impossible for a sponsor to tell the press the simplest fact
without floating it in gallons of spirit, or burying it under
potato crisps. During the year, a newspaper sports depart-
ment receives about 250 invitations of this sort. The majority
go into the wastepaper basket. But the *Sunday Times* decided to
see what would happen if we accepted every one in a week.

For a pipe-opener, I choose a macabre champagne breakfast in the gloom of a Penthouse club tastefully decorated with
illuminated photographs of female loins. This is to launch the
Penthouse – Rizla – BAF 1977 Grand Prix racing car. I sit at a
table with two journalists just there for the grub. 'I don't know
why they invite us to these things,' complains one as he
washes down marmalade with champagne. 'We never print
anything. Typical British PR if you ask me.'

An official appeals for questions from the journalists, most
of whom are by now wondering whether champagne will mix
with luke-warm kippers.

'How much will it cost?'

They refuse to say. Pressed, a spokesman says: 'Considerably more than last year.'

'How much did it cost last year?'

'Considerably less than this year,' booms a drunken voice.
Laughter.

There are no more questions.

The champagne ceases suddenly as the Penthouse girls go
outside for the real business of the day, a photograph of the car

draped with females, and blinking in the sunlight the press shamble away.

This is followed by Horror Day – three receptions in one lunchtime. The gin flows freely at the Lawn Tennis Association as they tell us about the ATP Grand Prix qualifying singles – what used to be the Beckenham Tennis Week in happier days – but I've only time for seven or eight before I dash to the Football Association HQ for a reception by the Women's FA, who apparently just want to make the press happy. This is sponsored by Pony, the Drink with a Kick, who have thoughtfully left free bottles of the stuff all over the place. I drain a couple. It does indeed have a kick.

Outside, Lancaster Gate is rocking gently in the sunlight, and the pavement sways up and down as I hail a taxi by the simple process of staggering in front of it. From somewhere near the bumper I call imperiously to the driver, 'Take me immediately to the Havoy Sotel!' He does so and helps me through the revolving door as I seem to have difficulty in doing this myself.

At the Savoy, the Colgate-Palmolive Freestyle Skiing Championships are holding an intimate lunch for reporters to meet four beautiful American girl skiers, and good fortune and Colgate-Palmolive place me next to the lovely Suzy Chaffee, who was once pictured nude on skis in the *Sunday Times*, and who preaches the philosophy of Love Your Body and Let It All Hang Out, Man.

The gins and the Ponys are joined by a couple of large camparis and a quart or so of Châteauneuf du Pape. The fumes rise to where the brain would be in a non-journalist. Miss Chaffee looks unutterably desirable in her tight-fitting light blue romper-suit. I move closer. She leans towards me. Suddenly she squeezes my arm affectionately and says: 'When was the last time you gave someone you love a massage all over?'

The headline fantasies weave around my Châteauneuf-du-Pape-sodden brain.

BEAUTIFUL GIRL SKIER
TELLS OF AFFAIR WITH
SPORTS WRITER

Incredible Potency

Like an Animal in Bed
Massaged All Over

My head sinks drunkenly over the tablecloth until it is about three inches from Miss Chaffee's beautiful bosom. There is a gentle tinkling noise, as of ice dropping into a glass. Miss Chaffee is talking.

'Michael,' she says. 'Do you know I have been to a doctor, and taken one of those tests they do in Sweden, and they tell me I have a biological age of only fifteen.'

'You could have fooled me,' I mutter into the tablecloth, and then reluctantly pull myself together. Miss Chaffee may have a biological age of fifteen, but mine at the moment feels like seventy five.

In fact, my hangover is so powerful it lasts until the next day, which is unfortunate, as I have been invited to take gin with Eley Ammunition at some damp meadow in Rickmansworth that morning, and to blaze away freely. I wake with a head that feels as if a press reception were being held inside it, and an apprehension that it is rather dangerous to hand out shotguns to thirty gin-sodden journalists ('I tell you wash, ol' man, you put your gin and tonic on your head, and I'll shoot it off'). Every bang goes through my head like a spike, but I return whole, having hit two clay pigeons out of twelve, and even they gave themselves up. I lunch on gin, brandy and crisps.

By next day I have developed a terrible heartburn. A potato crisp must have become permanently lodged in the gullet, so I don't care that I have a diary entry for 11 a.m. which I can't read. Somewhere they are swilling gin and eating crisps and I am not there, and I am glad, glad, glad.

Thus I arrive for the Ford Motor reception in a bad temper but the affair proves quite informative. Smooth and professional, it includes a phone link with driver Roger Clarke in Nairobi. A delicious lunch, however, is wrecked by the crisp in my gullet, which now appear to have burst into flames. What shall it profit a man if he gain a whole free lunch and a duodenal ulcer?

'They tell me I have a biological age of 15'

I've been prejudiced against horses ever since I served as a trooper in the 7th Hussars, so I attend the British Show Jumping Association lunch in a vile mood with my pencil ready to write about chinless wonders in jodhpurs and purple-faced ex-colonels and all that sort of thing, but they are utterly charming and questions are answered with such frankness that I forget the pain in my chest, helped by five glasses of vintage port. I stagger away at 3.30 and return to the office where I fall asleep in the lift.

However, by six o'clock I am in the Tom Cribb public house, near Haymarket, to meet Alan Lloyd, author of *The Great Prize Fight*. It's an unusual reception, just three or four people including the author and Henry Cooper and myself, jammed in a public bar while Cassells pay for the drinks. By eight o'clock I am awash, and catch my tube train. But I have to get out two stations early, as I feel sick.

After this, I determine not to drink *anything* at the All-England Badminton Championships at Wembley, but on arrival, behold! there are the free gins all lined up winking at me, and it is all too much. Once more I dine on gin and crisps. I see no badminton. This time I get on a train going in the wrong direction.

Eventually it all ends. I gain several pounds in weight during the week, which is just about equal to the weight of paper I collect, most of it bearing useless information such as the fact that Rizla cigarette papers were founded in 1799 (doubtless by Napoleon). I also have forty cigarettes, three badges, a notebook and a thing to stop your car smelling, which doesn't work. I shall need an operation to remove the burning pain in my gullet.

As a result of my experiences I should like to suggest yet another Writer of the Year award. It would go to the journalist who had survived the most press receptions. It would be sponsored by a gin company with help from a manufacturer of potato crisps. And I would be the first winner.

5

Box and Cox

We take affluence in sport for granted these days, and only the other week I heard of a spoiled young rugby star who wouldn't play until his club provided him with a new pair of boots. So it may seem difficult to believe, but when we started up an office cricket team soon after the Second World War no one possessed a bat or a pad between them. Perhaps it isn't so surprising when it's remembered most of us had just come out of the Services, having gone in as little more than boys. Any gear we might have possessed had vanished, rotted or apparently shrunk in our absence. We were also employees of what I firmly believe was the meanest local newspaper in western Europe.

Despite this, our first act was to elect the Editor as President; the second to demand a fiver of him. Much to our surprise he gave it to us, although three weeks later he said it was only a loan and he wanted it back, so we had to raffle a ham to raise the money.

Money went a lot further in those times, so with the fiver, and our own contributions, we were able to purchase two bats, four pads, two sets of batting gloves, two sets of stumps, two balls and one protective box. This was the essential minimum of equipment needed, except in the matter of the box, where we really ought to have had two, one for each batsman, but our money had run out at that point.

Luckily we didn't need the box for the first fixture, which was played on a shirt-front park wicket against a team of gentle little tailors and market traders, the Jewish Ex-Servicemen's Association, the only side I ever know whose opening bowler was so slow that sometimes the ball didn't even reach the wicket. In any case pace bowlers on either side would have been hampered by the fact that they wore braces. We won convincingly and, swollen with pride, fixed up another match against a village in west Northamptonshire.

Pride came before the fall. This was a 'proper' fixture against a side who possessed a terrible fast bowler known locally as The Crusher, a giant farm labourer who literally foamed and salivated all over the pitch with the effort of hurling down his thunderbolts.

Hearing of The Crusher's reputation, our opening batsman claimed The Club Protector as his right and retired behind the hedge to put it on, there being no pavilion. It was an old-fashioned device, left over from pre-war stock I suspect, designed for wicket-keepers, and large and clumsy, about the size and shape of a soup tureen. It had already been nick-named Cromwell, after the Lord Protector. When our man re-appeared he was walking with a strange gait that suggested an internal injury, and after a brief discussion he retired to put it on the right way round. Then battle commenced.

The Crusher began his run right from the ditch at the end of the field, and arrived at the wicket hurling saliva in all directions. His first ball was so fast it was almost invisible and our opener, a half-blind lad with thick spectacles who specialized in reporting films, stared paralysed until the ball smote him in the groin with a terrible clang (The Box being made of metal), and he sank to the ground, moaning. But he was soon pulled to his feet by our treasurer, who ran out to see if The Protector had been damaged.

There was a bye off the next ball. This brought the Chief Reporter to face The Crusher. But just as the bowler was winding up for his run he called out, 'Do you mind waiting, old man, while we exchange The Box?' and the game was held up while the two batsmen met in mid-wicket and groped round their private parts. As they kept scoring in singles – mostly in byes – and changed The Protector each time, it was the longest over ever bowled – nearly twenty minutes if memory serves me right. It was too much for their skipper, who at the end of it removed The Crusher from bowling and the match was able to proceed without the necessity for exchanging The Box after each run.

After being soundly defeated we came to leave, and couldn't find The Box. Eventually, we had to go without it, with much moaning about the expense of equipment these days. But next year, one of our reporters, cycling through the village, discovered it. The Lord Protector was in The Crusher's front garden, filled with earth and sprouting hyacinths. We deemed it tactful to leave him in possession.

6

Max Boyce's Cousin

One of the people connected with rugby I very much admire is
Max Boyce, the Welsh entertainer who has made an international reputation by becoming the world's first rugby folk-
singer and winner of a golden disc. After I had written some
material for a television programme in which Max also
appeared, he suggested I should write something especially for
him, so I did so. Alas, it didn't work quite work out smoothly.
The idea Max suggested was that I should write a letter for
him to read from an imaginary English cousin, taking the
mickey out of English rugby. So I wrote a piece which did this,
but which also poked fun at the Welsh as well. Max rang up to
say, 'That was absolutely smashing that piece you sent, but I
hope you didn't mind, *I've knocked out all the anti-Welsh jokes.*'
The result was that when Max came to the TV broadcast I
felt like someone who's just been paid to betray their own
nation. To make matters worse, Max began the piece by
screwing a monocle into his eye and spoke in an English
accent which can only be described as like something out of
The Lives of a Bengal Lancer. After the recording, Jack Williams,
the producer, put an arm round my shoulder and said, 'I have
to tell you, Michael, that we need to cut five minutes from the
show and it so happens your number was exactly five minutes
long. . . .' Thus it never did make the screen, but Max was so
determined to get it right that he worked on it for weeks after,
and finally tried a revised performance in a live show in the
valleys, where it was a triumphant success once he reverted to
his own Welsh accent.

Here, then, is the original version of the pieces written for

Max, with the jokes about the Welsh carefully re-assembled and put back by myself:

'MAX: I wonder if you'd forgive me if I make use of the programme for a personal appeal. You see I've had a rather urgent letter from my cousin Tarquin in England and I'd like to read it to you.

'Dear Max,

I wonder if you could do me a favour, knowing the influence you have in Wales. I am writing now both as a relative and an official of the Old Rottinghamians Rugby Football Club. As you know, on the morning of last international we entertained a team from Wales. It was quite a good game, if somewhat over-vigorous on the part of the visitors, but unfortunately when they returned to Wales they took with them quite a lot of our clubhouse. I particularly wish to appeal for the return of our dressing-room mirror, the chairman's portrait and our crossbar. In addition, we wish to know the name of the Welsh player who dropped his sock in the tea-urn. This can now only be used for coffee. But most important of all, we would like to appeal for the return of our President. He was last seen staggering on to the Welsh coach with his arm round a seventeen-year-old girl. The President's wife is deeply distressed as she does not know what to tell the golf club.

Also, could you recommend a more respectable club for this fixture in the future? I am not a snob, but after we had laid on a special lunch for the Welsh side we found most of it plastered over the bust of our Founder-member. I must admit it was a mistake to serve curry, especially as the chairman of our Ladies' Committee, Mrs Barnstaple, informs me it was accidentally over-cooked, and had to be prised from the saucepan with a screwdriver and then cut into chunks with a bread-saw. However, that does not excuse the behaviour of one of the Welsh side who wrapped a piece in newspaper and later threw it at a Rugby Union official who tried to stop him tying a leek on the posts. The missile struck the official in the stomach and severely winded him.

That is all for now. As our Welsh visitors would say, *'Cymru am byth'* which I understand means, 'Hullo, little saucepan.' What a strange nation!

Yours sincerely,
TARQUIN'

Another letter from Tarquin was written for the next programme:

'Dear Max,

You remember in my last letter I appealed for the return of our elderly President, who was last seen staggering on to our Welsh visitor's coach with his arm round a young girl. Well, do not worry, we have got him back. He was found slumped by a petrol pump at the Severn Bridge Service Station with a road sign on his chest saying:

BEWARE OF ESCAPING GAS

Unfortunately, the President's wife has now asked us to take him back to Wales and dump him again. She says she does not know what went on while he was away, but after that evening he has become "like an animal in bed". She thinks this is disgusting in a man of sixty two, especially as they agreed to give up that sort of thing years ago. Now for the good news. You will be delighted to hear the club is running a trip to Cardiff to see the international with Scotland. We are going to play a really wizard jape on the Welsh crowd.

We are going to dress like Scotsmen and wear kilts in the Old Rottinghamian colours of red, white, blue and cerise. In addition, our Ladies Committee have knitted us matching underwear in case of accidents. We shall talk like Scotsmen, saying things like, "Och aye Jock, hold your wheest, deed to goodness Mac," and so forth. If we do this, no one will ever guess we are really English. I remember we once played a similar wheeze at Twickers and it worked very well except when a Scottish supporter poured whisky on to my sporran and then set it alight. This was a rather alarming experience, and at one time I thought I should have to go to the Marriage Guidance Council.

We shall bring with us our hooker's secretary, Dinah Morgan. She is a Welsh lady and she says if she can get a good look at the Cardiff committee box, she may recognize the father of her twenty-year-old son.

Best wishes,
TARQUIN'

7   *Trouble up the Creek*

I was pleased when asked to write on the somewhat obscure subject of anchors, because there won't be many more chances to do so. Marinas are springing up so fast the anchor is falling into disuse, and there are plenty of yachtsmen who go from spring to autumn without every unshipping that crooked trouble-maker in the bows. This is a pity, because it's only the anchor that lets you enjoy the pleasures of those little creeks away from the busy harbours and marinas. It is also the anchor which provides more unusual and less pleasant experiences, such as the occasion when I went to sleep anchored in a little bay off Sark, and woke up in the middle of the night to find myself actually inside a cave. For two minutes I was firmly convinced I'd died in the night.

My first experience of anchoring should have warned me of the dangers. I was on a troopship, a terrible old tub of a Liberty ship, which broke down in the Solent and anchored for repairs to the engine. When they'd completed these they tried to raise the anchor with the result there was a terrible grating noise and the ship nearly turned over. They'd hooked the main electricity cable from the mainland. At the time I roared with laughter but now I wouldn't find it so funny, having myself slipped cables and generously donated anchors to the beds of numerous creeks from Bosham to Poole.

One of the troubles about anchoring is that people talk as if it's the easiest thing in the world, using phrases like, 'Sling your hook,' which suggest casually taking a small object about the size of a door handle and dropping it overboard, whereas we all know that dropping the anchor on a small craft is much more like rodding the drains.

I remember seeing a fit, cheerful, young member of the crew go forward to drop the anchor on a twenty two ft sloop once. It wasn't anywhere dangerous – the middle of Poole Harbour to be exact, although it was dark.

We'd done our usual trick and got cold feet about going to France even before we'd left the harbour, and decided to anchor until the weather moderated.

After he'd left the well, there were a series of strange noises from up front and ten minutes later a broken, gibbering Thing crawled back along the cabin roof.

As we were drifting at what felt like ten knots towards Brownsea Island we urgently asked him, 'What about the anchor?' and he replied, ' —— the anchor, I've broken my leg.'

The facts were that he had the usual trouble with an anchor in the dark, getting it entangled with the jib, the forestay and anything else within reach, and finally lost his temper, pushed it under the pulpit and hurled it overboard wildly, only to feel a terrible seizure of his ankle, round which he had apparently managed to wind the chain in his confusion.

'The only thing that stopped me going overboard,' he said dramatically, 'was the fact that my foot was too big to go through the fairhead.'

Like most yachtsmen he was, of course, an unmentionable liar, but there was no doubt his ankle was badly bruised so we rowed ashore and took him to hospital where they deflated us all by describing the accident on their report as, 'bruised ankle while playing'.

That young man was, in fact, the second person I have seen reduced to a gibbering idiot by an anchor. The other was a girl and she was raising it, although I think it's rather a strain for a girl. However, she was doing splendidly when she gave a sudden shriek and jumped back into the well, speechless. Thinking the harbourmaster had been exposing himself again, I went forward and found what appeared to be a shrivelled human hand wedged in the chain. It was, in fact, a white rubber glove, and its sudden appearance over the side had been too much for the poor girl. Rather tactlessly, I threw it back to the cockpit with a cry of, 'There you are, there's

It was, in fact, a white rubber glove

nothing to worry about,' and this time she nearly jumped overboard.

Most of my anchor memories seem to be fraught with fear, like the time I was awoken as we sailed down the Thames Estuary by a terrible roar like an express train passing by, to find the anchor had slid overboard; or the occasion when I awoke while anchored in Wootton Creek to hear a gentle tapping on the side of the boat and discovered it was caused by a large steel spike sticking out of the water, over which we had moored.

But it's not always like that, of course. To those who spend their sailing trips going from marina to marina I'd say, try crawling up some little creek and taste the joys of a night at anchor. You have nothing to lose except a good night's sleep.

8 *An Appeal from the Golf Coarse*

The news that the BBC are to do another *Play Golf* series filled me with horror. We don't need any more cheap propaganda encouraging people to play the blasted game, what's desperately needed is some advice on how to give it up. What hope is there for young people today when they are subjected to evil rubbish of this kind by what is supposed to be a responsible public corporation?

I myself have been struggling to give up golf for fifteen years. For at least fourteen of those years I have got no better, and if anything slightly worse. I belong to that great army of Coarse Golfers, who go from tee to green without touching the fairway, whose idea of a good round is when they lose only five balls or break only one club. Yet like all the other poor fools, I am sustained by the fallacy that the next stroke, the next hole, the next round, is going to be better.

Like a smoker, I am well aware of the harm I am doing to myself, without being able to stop it. It is a monstrous lie that golf is good for you. It encourages gambling and drinking to excess; it makes one introverted and obsessed with figures; it is ruinously expensive; it makes a man (and a woman) neglect his family; and it has a terrible effect on the character, so that the sufferer gets his values all wrong, pays no attention to the real world about him and can think only of winning the monthly medal or reducing his handicap or even just getting a handicap.

When a golfer says a terrible tragedy has happened, he doesn't mean his family have been killed in a blazing home, he

means he's missed an eighteen-inch putt or has started to
shank.

There is an old golf legend about a player who saw a funeral
procession pass along the road as he was putting. He instantly
stopped, stood to attention and took off his hat. When his
partner asked why, he replied, 'Well, she'd been a good wife to
me for thirty years.' Unfortunately, that story is a slight
understatement, if anything. In real life, he would have continued to play.

The passions aroused by obsession with golf can break
lifelong friendships, even split up families. My friend Askew
always claimed his failure in life was due to playing golf with
his boss in a vital match. It all depended on the last hole.
Askew strode to the tee, determined to make the biggest drive
of his life. Unfortunately, in his hysterical vigour he missed the
ball completely and his momentum caused him to slide off the
raised tee into some bushes ('I flew through the air like a dart,'
said Askew dramatically, but I think he was exaggerating).

My most determined effort to give up golf came after the
police called at my house one evening holding a golf ball, and
asked, 'Is this yours, sir?'

'Yes,' I said. 'I think it is. It's jolly decent of you to go to all
this trouble to return it. People are wrong when they say the
police aren't what they used to be. Was it the one I sent into
the allotments?'

'No,' said the sergeant. 'It was the one you hit through the
windscreen of a number sixty-five bus.'

An interesting conversation followed, lasting about an hour.
The police couldn't believe I didn't know what had happened
to the ball, which had vanished off the toe of the driver on the
thirteenth tee.

'Didn't you search for it, sir?'

'Search? I didn't even know in which direction it had gone.'

'Surely, sir, you must have known whether it went left or
right, or backwards or forwards?'

'Not necessarily, officer. It is obvious you know very little
about golf.'

'One might say the same about you, sir.'

I know what this golf TV programme is going to be like.

Someone will come up to a ball and hit it all wrong and then lo, behold the genial professional will come along and hit it all right and show the man what to do, and everyone will smile and realize how easy it is. And it will be all LIES, LIES, LIES.

What we want is a programme entitled *Don't Play Golf*, showing the truth about the wretched game. This programme would portray all the things *Play Golf* won't show, starting off with a shot of howling infants crying, 'Where is my Daddy?' We would see a man hit a ball against a tree and watch it bounce back sixty yards. We would watch four players quarrelling bitterly over the interpretation of some local rule about balls which land in sheep droppings. We would see film of respectable middle-aged women crawling around in thistles in the rain, looking for balls. We would see someone making a shot just like the genial pro did and dancing around in agony as he digs the club deep into the ground and sprains his wrist. Above all, we would see sequences of family breadwinners paying five pounds for a round; handing over £7.50 to their opponents in side-bets; and then going into the pro's shop and forking out £10 for a metal stick with a lump on the end, known as a club.

It would undoubtedly win an international award for the BBC as documentary of the year. And I would volunteer to write the script myself, if I wasn't so busy playing golf three times a week.

'Well, she'd been a good wife to me for thirty years'

9 Squire Haggard in the Field

Squire Haggard, the central figure of my book *Squire Haggard's Journal*, was an imaginary eighteenth-century squire, who represented everything that was vile about a period which was plagued with diarists recording the dismal details of their grim lives and their frequent debaucheries. Squire Haggard knew little of sport, except for hunting and wenching, but he had many of the characteristics of a Coarse Sportsman, notably in his fondness for drinking himself into a stupor on every possible occasion. I thought it would be interesting to write what might have happened if he had ever been brought into contact with two eighteenth-century sporting occasions:

JULY 13, 1778: Rain. Amos Bindweed to be hanged for stealg. a farthg. Chas. Fundament d. from Seizg. of the Bowels. Whilst chasg. a wounded poacher towards Long Bottom I encountered an alarmg. spectacle, viz., sevl. villagers in a state of undress hurlg. balls at one another and wavg. wooden staves in the air. Presumg. this to be preparation for a Jacobite rebellion or a Papist plot I gave them a blast from my fowlg. piece, and rode for Col. Fuse of The Militia, shoutg., 'Long Bottom has risen against the Throne!' But I was halted by a cry that they were only practisg. for a cricket match. Percvg. this indeed to be the case I learned that the game is this week against Vulture-sub-Underwood.

JULY 14, 1778. Mist. To town to see Amos Bindweed hanged, he owg. me 0£ 0s. 1¼d. Chas. Fundament buried in wrong grave. Recvd. from Obadiah Moon the sum of

0£ 0s. 2¾d., the farthg. being a bad one. Shot interestg. poacher in p.m. and dined with Sir Josh Faggott, who wagered 500 sovs. that Vulture-sub-Underwood will win the cricket match tomorrow. Drank five botts. of Madeira and carried home strapped to the roof of my coach, the servants being unable to get me inside.

JULY 15, 1778. Cloud. Amos Bindweed found to be innocent. Chas. Fundament dug up and reburied in right grave. Jas. Trumpet d. from Gripg. of the Guts. Up early and to Long Bottom for the cricket match. Vulture-sub-Underwood batted first and achieved 130 notches, chiefly through Sir Josh's half-witted son Horatio, whom nobody would bowl out or catch out for fear of offendg. his father, who owns most of the village. He was thus permitted to bat for five hours, those of the fielders who were his father's tenants offerg. to bowl the ball wherever he desired, and he still not able to hit it properly. His inngs. only terminated when he put his foot in a rabbit hole whilst runng. between the wickets and was carried from the field with a broken ankle.

When Long Bottom batted they soon made 129 notches for the loss of only three batsmen, as the Vulture-sub-Underwood team have no good bowlers, their best man, Shooter Jackson, hvg. just been hanged for stealg. a sheep. It seemed certain I must win my wager and I approached Sir Josh for the money when I saw an astonishg. spectacle, viz., two strong footmen lifted up his injured son and carried him to the wicket from which position he began to bowl whilst the footmen supported him. Immediately all the Long Bottom batters, being afraid of offendg. a gentln., surrendered their wickets, doffg. their hats, touchg. their forelocks and cryg. 'God bless you young sir.' Some deliberately gave catches, whilst three kicked down their wickets and cried, 'Well bowled young Mr. Horatio, you are a chip off the old block.' And so they lost by one run and I went home the poorer by 500 sovs., ventg. my wrath by horsewhippg. a Dissenter I met on the road. ITEM: To horsewhip, 0£ 0s. 2½d.

OCT. 4, 1778. Hail. Bart. Seedcake d. from a General Put-

refaction. Job Muckraker struck dead whilst eatg. his dinner.
Flogged elderly servant in a.m. with unwonted vigour and in
p.m. dined with Sir Josh Faggott. Being unable to move I was
also constrained to stay to supper, where I drank eight botts.
of port, and six labourers carried me home on a sheep hurdle.
ITEM: to labourers 0£ 0s. 4d.

OCT. 5, 1778. Thunder. Job Muckraker refused christian
burial. Prudence Peascod d. from the Mange. Awoke with a
violent headache caused by an excess of the black humour. To
my surprise I was clutchg. in my hand a wager for 1,000£ with
Sir Josh to the followg. effect, viz., that Long Bottom would
beat Vulture-sub-Underwood tomorrow in the Great Annual
Knurdlg. match. Since Vulture-sub-Underwood have won the
Knurdle for seven years in succession I realized that Sir Josh.
had imposed upon me whilst I was drunk.

OCT. 6, 1778. Rain. Dissenters agree to bury Job Muckraker.
Enoch Turncoat d. from Putrefaction of the Lights. Evicted
Granny Bradshaw in a.m. and at noon large crowds arrived
for the Knurdlg., in which a barrel of beer containg. 47⅔
pints is hurled into a stream midway between the two villages,
and the young men of each village then try to push it to their
opponents' village, usg. only their noses, or Knurdles as they
are known locally.

The Knurdlg. began on the stroke of twelve, and by five
o'clock the men of Vulture-sub-Underwood were within 10
yards of the Long Bottom parish pump, their superiority being
due to their exceptionally large noses, which are prepared for
the Knurdle by being hardened with linseed oil. Realizg. my
1000£ was in the direst jeopardy, I spoke to my bailiff, and just
as the men of Vulture-sub-Underwood were about to Knurdle
the cask for the last time he rushed through the crowd shoutg.
'Protect your homes! Vulture-sub-Underwood is on fire from
end to end!', whereupon the Knurdlers rushed back to the
village and the Long Bottom men at once took possession of
the cask and drank the contents, thus renderg. the contest void
and themselves insensible. ITEM: To bribes 0£ 1s. 3¼d.

'*Vulture-sub-Underwood is on fire from end to end!*'

10 When Truth is Funnier than Fiction

Or Why the Priest Winced While Saying Mass

One of the problems of being an allegedly humorous writer is that truth is not only stranger than fiction, it's usually a darn sight funnier too. The 'funny' author, such as myself, desperately raises his literary sledgehammer and produces a tinkle; the 'straight' writer taps his fingernail on the bell of life and a great peal rings out. I write as one of whom the *Sheffield Telegraph* said many years ago, 'Put another record on, Mr Green, we are tired of the old one.' I sympathize with that critic. I know the feeling. But at least he read the book, which is more than the critic of *The Scotsman* did. He just copied out the publisher's blurb, which described me as the funniest thing to hit literature since Kit Marlow, or words to that effect, and that appalling untruth has been plastered all over my books ever since immediately under the original blurb, like this:

We believe Michael Green has never been funnier or more depressingly accurate.

'Michael Green has never been funnier or more depressingly accurate' – *The Scotsman*

Two books I once reviewed for *Punch* illustrate the point about truth in humour perfectly. One was a deliberately funny book by a well-known writer on how to treat women, and despite the elaborate professional care with which it was constructed I hardly smiled. The other book was a fairly straightforward historical study of some of the eccentric nobility who have graced this country in the past and contained an incredible description of the death of the Duke Ormonde. The good

Duke, asking to be helped to a chair, said to his host, a German baron: 'Excuse me sir, if I make some grimaces in your presence, but my physician tells me I am at the point of death.' The baron courteously replied: 'Ah, my lord Duke, I hope you will not put yourself under any constraint on my account.'

It's difficult to cap that sort of thing by *inventing* something funny. Especially when the author later described an eighteenth-century Duke of Somerset who hated the common people so much he had outriders scouring the countryside to stop them staring at him (a farm labourer cunningly hid behind a hedge, however, and held a pig up to him as he rode by).

As I said in an earlier chapter, I've always found that the most bizarre sporting stories aren't those that are invented, but the true ones. No sooner do I write a book with a few funny reminiscences then truth starts catching up as new incidents which are even more unbelievable come to notice. Take the case of Old Brentwoods RFC. Few things in *The Art of Coarse Rugby* could equal their experience, unique surely in any game, of setting out from the dressing-room with fifteen men and losing four on the way to the pitch, so they had to start four short? Apparently the field is five miles away down country lanes and the missing four were in a car which got lost. The same club also tell me gleefully that once when they were short the opposition lent them a player who was promptly sent off for kicking one of his own club-mates.

Then there was the strange case of Father M. J. Blackburn, an Irish priest, who was following the noblest traditions of his Faith by playing in the second row of London Irish Extra B. Father Blackburn was chosen to say prayers at a service at the club when they scattered the ashes of Fitz (George Fitzpatrick), the immortal character who gave his name to the famous Fitz's bar, over which he presided. This was an insanitary but cosy wooden hut, one of the last of the old-time London rugby bars, which hosted generations of players from all over the world until it was closed and torn down in 1975, soon after which Fitz died. His ashes were scattered where the old bar had stood.

However, it was not so much that which gained Fr. Blackburn the attention of the national press, but the fact that a few weeks later he had to drop out of the Extra B with surely the most bizarre excuse for not playing ever heard. He claimed he slipped a disc while taking off his vestments after reading Mass. Following that, his captain told him to choose between Mass and rugby, and he chose the Church, a great loss to the game.

Along with Fr. Blackburn in Rugby's Hall of Fame should go D. D. Dobson, who played in three Varsity matches at the turn of the century and then went out to Nyasaland, where he had the misfortune to be killed by a charging buffalo. According to the late Ross McWhirter and Sir Andrew Noble in their *Centenary History of the OURFC*, when the news was broken to the games master at his old school, that gentleman commented, 'Ah yes, Dobson always did have a weak hand-off.'

Many extraordinary stories appear in the form of deadpan snippets from local papers, such as the one from Hampshire:

Winchester RFC 'A' XV were without the services of their veteran hooker Bertram last week, as he was suffering from sore knees following the annual dinner-dance.

Another cutting in front of me is from the *Irish Times* and under the bland heading UNHAPPY AFTERNOON FOR REFEREE it tells how Ken Dexter, officiating in Lansdowne *v.* Trinity, first of all had to cope with the problem that at one end gales had blown down the crossbar and one upright. It was a rough game and several players were injured, says the report. But 'the referee suffered the worst injury of all when he collided with a player and sustained a fractured jaw bone'. To make matters worse, the injury apparently came as he was running into position to judge a conversion kick. When he recovered consciousness one touch judge had his flag up and the other was signalling 'no goal'. It was not revealed how he coped with that embarrassing situation, especially as he was now unable to speak.

From Sussex I am sent a cutting headed:

TOUCHLINE DRAMA AS PLAYER GETS MARCHING ORDERS FROM SKIPPER

This read as follows:

Even the top of Caterham Hill was muddy on Saturday and only one of the pitches belonging to the Old Caterhamians Rugby Club could be used; so East Grinstead Extra B team had to travel a mile from the welcoming clubhouse to a well-grassed pitch but spartan changing-rooms.

It was from this long shed-like building that just after the interval emerged a heavily-built figure carrying a hold-all. His emergence was to some extent a distraction to those Old Caterhamians not immediately occupied with the ball. Looking neither to left nor right the burly figure crossed the edge of the pitch and came to the halfway line. Here he stopped and dramatically faced the game. He opened his hold-all and scattered his rugby togs, jersey, shorts, stockings, boots and everything else a rugby player takes comfort from, on the ground. Then shaking the mud from his upturned bag he stalked from the field, never looking back.'

The aggrieved player had, apparently been sent off by his own skipper a quarter of an hour earlier for bad language and for querying the decisions of the referee.

Another cutting sent by some unknown connoisseur of Coarse Rugby, concerns Jonathan Wilson, aged fifteen, who set what is believed to be a world record when he made his playing debut for two different clubs in the same game.

Wilson, a Millfield schoolboy, turned up for Dorchester A XV's game against Tiverton. It was his first appearance and he was directed to the wrong dressing-room, where Tiverton, who were a man short, assumed he had been sent to play for them. So Wilson trooped on to the field with the visitors and played nearly a full first half for Tiverton before Dorchester realized what had happened and he was asked, 'Shouldn't you be playing for us?'

He duly changed shirts during half-time and finished the game with Dorchester, the result being a 20–20 draw. Afterwards he said, 'I wish people would make up their bloody minds.'

Sometimes old friends remind one of personal experience you've forgotten. Like the people at Walsall who reminded me of the time when my brother Roger, while playing against them for Stoneygate in the 1950s, laid out an old Walsall enemy during a fierce maul. 'Who did that?' the referee asked Walsall. 'Someone must have seen it.' But there came no answer and play went on. Afterwards in the bar the referee

asked Walsall why they didn't tell him that Roger Green had
flung the fatal punch. 'Because you'd have sent him off'
came the reply. 'And then we couldn't have got revenge on
him in the second half.'

A letter from Alcester RFC tells of their tour of Majorca,
where the team couldn't understand their blinding hangovers
after only a few gin and tonics until they saw the barman draw
off a slug of the gin, which was made locally, pour it on a rag
and use it to clean the grease off his gleaming coffee machine.
After that they stuck to beer.

I made much in *The Art of Coarse Rugby* about elderly players
still tottering around in the Extra B, but the true-life story of
my old friend Ken Bonner beats any fiction hollow. A year or
two back he was still a member of the front row of the Old
Elizabethans (Barnet) 5th XV at the ripe old age of sixty
three. Not only that, but the previous year the combined ages
of the front-row had been 187, with another sixty three-year
old prop and a fifty one-year -old hooker, but the other prop
retired.

Ken didn't even play rugby until he was thirty, when he
had a few wartime games in the Navy at an age when most
men are thinking of retirement. Afterwards he played for the
RNVR and Ealing.

He later played for Barnet, but in 1969 they refused to pick
him any more as they were scared he would drop dead on the
field and, in the words of a Barnet official, 'This would have
caused insurance complications.'

I can understand Barnet's feelings, because we used to
think the same when Ken played with me for Ealing 3rd XV,
and in those days he was only in his forties. Even at that
comparatively youthful time he had a distressing habit of
foaming at the mouth throughout the entire game and groaning as he panted for breath. Opponents were scared to tackle
him in case they finished him off and respectfully stood aside
as he wheezed down the field, the more religious crossing
themselves. However, that wasn't often, as he had the hallmark of a true coarse rugger player and never travelled in the
same direction as the ball. After each scrum or line-out he
ignored the ball completely and simply headed for where he

though the next scrum or line-out would take place, so as to save unnecessary running, leaving a trail of foam on the ground. His son played in the same team and spent most of his time assuring everyone Dad wouldn't drop dead, he always made a noise like that.

Ken never trained in the conventional sense, but attributed his rugby longevity to regular horse-riding and beer.

Amateur drama is one of my 'sports' and I often wish I could convince people you don't have to make up stories about what happens on-stage, you just need a notebook. Alas, I had already written *The Art of Coarse Acting* when I saw a real-life happening that would have fitted into it perfectly.

I was watching a village drama group perform a rather dated play in the church hall. The play, which had been quite popular in the thirties, concerned an explorer on some jungle expedition, who fell seriously ill and was proving a handicap to the others' survival. Alone in his tent one evening, he decided to shoot himself to give the others a chance of reaching civilization safely.

The set showed the interior of the tent. The other explorers left ('Goodbye old chap, sleep well, we'll think of something in the morning . . . my God, but the insects are terrible, Fanshaw . . .'). When all was quiet the injured man crawled out of his blankets and painstakingly dragged himself to the tent pole, where his revolver was hanging. With agonizing slowness he reached up for the pistol with trembling hands.

Just as his clutching fingers seized it, the unfortunate actor loudly broke wind.

There was a moment's silence and then a great shout of laughter from the audience. They were still laughing when he shot himself, which was just as well, as the noise drowned the fact that the gun didn't go off.

Finally, as a last example of truth beating fiction, here is a notice from the board of a golf club in Middlesex:

'Last week my husband broke 90 for the first time in his life. If there are any members who have not had a detailed description of his round, would they please ring 01–475–4647 for a stroke-by-stroke account.'

11   Disco Train's Maiden Journey

The following is an account by me in the *Sunday Times* of an effort to control soccer hooliganism by providing a special supporter's train with all mod. cons.

Britain's most talked-about train, the Football League £250 000 Leagueliner Special, rolled into Euston station yesterday afternoon in the glare of TV lights. The fourteen-coach special, which the League hopes will prove an answer to hooliganism, brought 450 Burnley supporters up for the game against Queen's Park Rangers on its first trip.

All had gone well. No riots. No bovver. No broken windows. It could almost have been a Church Lads' Brigade outing or a Rotary Club special.

The Leagueliner has caught the public imagination and they've been talking about it in Burnley all week. In the Swan Hotel on Friday, two elderly gents in flat caps were discussing the train as if it were going to be a sort of mobile Gomorrah.

'They say,' said one, 'that they've got a special coach for the teenagers to do it in. With music provided an' all.'

'Ah don't see that,' said his mate. 'Ah mean – it stands to reason – they'd all fall over when bloody train goes round a bend.'

'They'll not fall over. They'll all be on't floor sinning with each other if Ah knows anything about young 'uns today.'

The reality proved different. Most of the 450 passengers on board took very seriously the printed notice they found on their seats from the Burnley team management reminding supporters that the 'eyes of the world' were on them.

That was nearly true. There must have been twenty five reporters and TV men on board. The sheer novelty, and the unaccustomed luxury of the first-class coaches seemed to overawe everyone at first as the train moved out of Burnley Central with Bob Lord, chairman of the Burnley club, in the driver's cab.

But as the team of twenty six volunteer stewards started to move down the train selling beer and coffee, the atmosphere thawed and the braver spirits began to sample the amenities. Of the fourteen first-class coaches, one had been converted into a disco car; two had piped music on headphones and one showed continuous colour TV (a two-month-old Arsenal *v.* Derby match).

With a loud noise like two skeletons sliding off a tin roof, the disco started up near Accrington, upsetting an old gentleman named Ernie who was using the toilet next door.

'I've never 'eard nowt like it in me life,' he complained. 'Well, not sitting on the toilet. I thought for a minute it must have been something I'd ate.'

'I told you to go before you came out,' said his wife.

But despite the attractions of a live, professional DJ with 500 records on tape, and psychedelic lighting, the garishly-painted disco car remained empty until the TV crews drove some teenagers in to be filmed. Just before Crewe there were only half a dozen girls dancing without boys watched by an enormous throng of some thirty *voyeurs* who seemed to have come in the hope of seeing some teenage sinning.

A slight verbal brush with a group of Manchester United supporters while waiting at Crewe provided a reminder of the Old Adam the train is intended to suppress, and from then on the train really began to come to life. The disco rocked with gyrating couples, none of whom, however, fell over, and who all remained severely chaste – on the train at least.

A fourteen-year-old girl wearing what appeared to be female bovver boots suddenly sat on my lap and demanded to be interviewed.

'You could tell them in the paper all about how I hit this Brighton supporter and got chased by twenty of their girls all the way to the station,' she said. 'Every time I go to a match me Dad searches me for weapons. He found a hammer on me once. He didn't 'alf create.'

Her friend, a lad of sixteen, complained that only stand tickets were available. 'I mean, some people want to go to the match for the fighting,' he said with complete seriousness.

But for one Burnley man the Leagueliner provided the experience of a lifetime. It was the first time he'd ever seen colour TV.

12 Turn N S W, Avoid Prams

The trouble with orienteering is Chris Brasher.

As one who admires the Olympic gold medallist I'd better explain that. I mean the sport suffers from an image given by tough runners like Brasher who've taken it up. In the public mind it has become identified with the limit-of-endurance brigade, the sort who want everybody to carry lead weights to make it more difficult.

But it isn't like that at all. It's one of the finest family sports ever invented and almost the only one where rabbits can compete with the olympians.

I was initiated by colleague Norman Harris, who simply invited me to dial a number, 01-242-2451. A recorded voice answered with news of all the orienteering events that weekend, together with map references of the venues. (Incidentally, why don't they do that in other sports? 'There are vacancies for forwards in Finchley fourth XV, three quarters in Ealing Extra C and Grasshoppers need a winger. . . .')

So I apprehensively arrived at a remote wood in Buckinghamshire and went through the formalities of buying a map and entering for a middle-range course. There was a choice of a dozen, from easy to impossible.

Now I am not the best of map-readers and in the Army I once guided a troop of tanks over a small precipice. ('They went like lemmings,' said an awed corporal.) As a yachtsman, I keep hitting the Isle of Wight every time I go to France. Even so, it was rather a surprise when I actually got lost on the start line.

You line up and, when a whistle is blown, run 150 yards to

I was cheered by the sight of a distraught schoolmaster

the master maps, from which you copy the location of the course control points on to your own map, and then rush off to find the first. Unfortunately, I dashed off in the opposite direction to everybody else and collided with the next lot of starters coming up, one of whom pointed out that my map was upside down.

However, my embarrassment was lessened by the presence of others who were not much more efficient, including school children, mums and dads, pensioners and at least one child in arms with the father carrying a push-chair. Some events allow prams.

They were clad in an astonishing variety of clothing. The only formality is that competitors must be covered, a rule introduced ever since someone suffering from hepatitis distributed the disease generously via the brambles. I was wearing a selection from the different sports at which I have failed in my life – rugby boots and socks, sailing trousers, cricket shirt, golf sweater. That's rather symbolic of orienteering. It's something like car rallying on foot, yachting through undergrowth

or playing golf without knowing where the greens are. The golfing analogy persists – one thinks of each leg as a 'hole'.

The first control was 600 yards away. It took me an hour to find it and I wasn't the slowest. Control is a misnomer – it's just a small sign on a tree with a clipper to punch your card and prove you've been there. For a time I thought I'd be the world's first orienteer to get a complete whitewash and then I literally stumbled upon it, slipping ten feet into a crevice where it was concealed. It was one of the great moments of my sporting career, like the time I managed to do the last hole at Wentworth in seven.

After that I got better. The next leg took a mere five minutes. Soon I was even being asked for advice by two schoolboys who were darting in all directions, uttering shrill yelps like lost dogs. I fear I may have misdirected them. They suddenly vanished over the edge of a deep gulley with howls of dismay.

But then, the woods were full of strange noises, from a heartfelt cry of, 'Daddy, where are you?' to the grunts of the limit-of-endurance lot, who squelched past with panting breath and lolling tongues, not speaking, unless someone got in their way.

Running was soon abandoned, but I plodded steadily round the course with only a few minor errors, such as when I reached control number 8 before number 6 and had to work backwards, followed by a young woman who was plainly lost, but whose presence merely led to excruciating discomfort, as I urgently wished to be alone to relieve myself (a serious problem in winter orienteering, when the undergrowth is thin).

At one stage a slavering Thing in a track suit rushed by and I recognized the distorted features of Norman Harris.

I became a little apprehensive when I'd been out for more than two hours; fog and darkness were creeping over the woods, and I'd finished the last of my brandy. But I was cheered by the sight of a distraught schoolmaster telling two boys to stay where they were and he'd come back and rescue them after he'd discovered where the others had got to. He loped off, leaving them standing pathetically like babes in the wood, clutching their maps.

And so to the finish. In the euphoria of completing the course I wobbled the last fifty yards, then pretended to collapse with cramp like Jim Peters in the marathon, and tottered in clawing the air and crying, 'Don't help me over the line!' They must have thought I was bonkers. I'd taken almost three hours to do just over five kilometres. Don't sneer, even the winner took fifty-three minutes.

My girl friend rushed out with coffee. She'd done the beginners' course, but she'd kept going round in circles and punched her card at the same control point three times.

The St John Ambulance people departed (only one customer, with a sprained foot, although they once had a case of hypothermia). Then they presented the prizes, all homemade. A vote of thanks for the landowner. Applause for the winning team. An appeal for someone to give a lift to a student. And then we all went home to tea. It seemed a long way from the crooked world of the Olympics. But this was sport, just the same.

13   *Woe to the Uncircumcised Batsman*

The BBC Woman's Hour programme once had the bright idea of inviting three speakers to take a biblical story and put it into modern times. One of the three people asked was me, and I decided to take the famous story of young David, who slew the giant Goliath with a stone from his sling, from the First Book of Samuel. This was the broadcast:

One of the greatest cricketing controversies for years, threatening even to surpass the bodyline row between England and Australia in 1932 has blown up over Surrey's application to register an eighteen-year-old Jewish lad named David Jesse. David, who saw action with the Jewish forces in the Middle East, has so far played in only two matches, but in each one he achieved the remarkable analysis of two overs, two maidens, ten wickets, no runs, all his wickets being cleaned bowled. Five of the batsmen were dismissed when the speed of the ball forced it straight through their bats. But it's not only David's speed which is sensational – a big controversy centres on his bowling methods, which are unorthodox to say the least. Instead of the conventional run-up he bowls from a standing position at the wicket, sending the ball down by wrapping it in his handkerchief and whirling it three times round his head. So far no one can find anything in the rules against this. The speed of his action makes close examination impossible, but the MCC intend to make a slow-motion film to see if his right elbow is straight at the moment of delivery.

Despite his sudden rise to fame, David is a quiet, modest lad who shares a flat in Hampstead with his close friend Jonathan. ('We are inseparable,' says Jonathan simply, 'but my father doesn't approve. I don't think he likes David.') But behind David's modest demeanour is a streak of toughness, and he admitted that he once killed a lion and a bear single-handed while on holiday in Israel. Perhaps it's this streak of toughness that causes him, before bowling, to shout at the batsman, 'Woe to the uncircumcised, this day will the Lord deliver thee into mine hand; and I shall smite thee.' Indeed, he admits that he was banned from playing cricket at school. 'There was this huge, big bully from another school who was hitting our chaps all over the place,' he said. 'Everyone was afraid of him, he was so big and fierce. So I volunteered to go on and bowl at him and my first ball hit him on the forehead and knocked him out.' But David says he has now cured his tendency to bowl at the head. Yet this remarkable young man's hobby is music, and he's an accomplished player on the harp, which he takes with him to every match. When I asked him if a harp wasn't rather bulky to carry about the country he replied simply, 'It's a Jew's harp.'

14 *The Curse of the Poison Dwarf*

When anyone asks me if I have ever been to Scotland, I usually reply absent-mindedly, 'no, only to Murrayfield.' Which is probably similar to the reply of most people who cross the Border for a rugby international and who wake up on Sunday morning to find they can remember nothing at all about the weekend except for the train journey on the way up. Actually, on this particular occasion it looked like being a reasonably sober weekend, as some fool on the rugby club committee had arranged a match on the morning of the international against a Scottish team, and despite all the jokes about it, playing rugby while drunk is no fun. I ought to know, I've done it often enough and it's fine for the first ten minutes, and then after that you're praying to be allowed to die quietly and as soon as possible.

So we were sober enough that morning and not very keen to play, what with being impatient to get to the international at Murrayfield. And it was cold, bitterly cold. It was so cold that Emrys Jones found his surgical support, which he had washed the night before, had frozen solid in the morning. He literally screamed with shock when he put it on but that's another story.

Now I like Scotsmen. As Billy Hughes, our hooker says, they taste better than Englishmen, and he should know, he's been sent off for biting four times. But no sooner was the ball in the air for the first line-out than I knew we were going to have trouble. I heard the voice of the dreaded Poison Dwarf from scrum-half. As is well known, the Poison Dwarf is a particular species of Scotsman remarkable for being just over

A poison dwarf

four feet tall, as aggressive and talkative as he is small, and impervious to pain. And there was one of these wee creatures lurking behind the Scottish forwards, and not treating things at all in the spirit of a morning game, where everyone agrees not to try too hard, but urging his forwards on with cries of, 'You're not going to let those bastards get away with that, are ye?' It was terrible.

Fortunately, his men totally failed to respond and the more they failed to trample on us, the more bitter and twisted he became. He even chased one of our players off the field. The poor chap went to hand off the Poison Dwarf, but he was so small that what was intended as a push in the chest hit him on the nose, and the Dwarf pursued him down the pitch crying that he would teach him to do that to Wee Jock McBlast or whatever his name was. They both vanished behind the pavilion and the Poison Dwarf returned, saying he'd chased him as far as the railway bridge and lost him in the traffic.

Mercifully, at this moment, the referee saw his car being towed away by the police, and promptly abandoned the game while he ran off to deal with the matter. When we got into the pub afterwards, I discovered a new thing about the Poison

Dwarf. He was even more aggressive when he was being friendly than when he was being nasty. He was terribly generous, pressing booze on to all and sundry, even when they didn't want it, but he was the only man I know who could make an invitation to a double Scotch sound like a personal challenge. No one dared to refuse. When we could hardly stand, the Poison Dwarf suggested that as you couldn't take drink into Murrayfield we should all meet for a round at a near-by hotel and he generously volunteered to go ahead and order up the drinks, which came to a rather extensive round as there were about twenty of us.

Well, to cut a long story short, he went to one hotel and our coach went by mistake to another and we didn't see the Poison Dwarf again until after the match, when we discovered him slumped against a wall on the Corstorphine Road, in what the police would call a dazed condition. 'Whatever happened?' we asked him.

'Well,' he said in a slurred voice. 'I ordered the drinks and when ye no turned up I decided not to waste them. And it takes a long time to drink six pints of beer, nine scotches, three gin and tonics and a vodka and tomato juice.'

15 Some Coarse Customers

One of the biggest myths in the world of drinking (a world which is inseparable from that of the Coarse Sportsman, who usually considers the drink afterwards more important than the game itself) concerns the ordinary public-house customer, who has been immortalized in prose and poetry by writers from Dickens to Chesterton as if a man became a totally different person the moment he walked into a public bar. The TV screen of course, lovingly perpetuates the myth with all those beer adverts full of happy people sinking pints and singing, when in reality they'd probably be moaning bitterly about life (see any City pub about 7.45 on a Monday evening – it's the most depressing place on earth).

Nowhere is this fallacy stronger than in country pubs, a subject which seems to bring out the worst in everyone, so that drinkers in the country are always discussed as if they were some sort of wise old peasant–philosophers, untouched by modern civilization, leading a life of kindliness and wisdom as they sip their rustic ale from the wood and gnaw their cheese. The truth of that impression can be ascertained any Sunday lunch-time in the country, where the prevailing sound will be not of church bells and rustic voices, but of motor-cycles, fruit machines, piped music and town voices.

One thing the telly doesn't mention about your English pub yokel is that he is incredibly mean. I used to play quoits in a remote Shropshire village. At first I didn't know the technicalities of the game, so the locals suggested we played for half a pint of beer each time, with the result that I was losing about eight pints a night. My opponents were stretched out all

Wise old peasant-philosophers

over the bar, drunk to the wide. Word quickly got round there was some idiot from the city throwing free booze away and they were queuing up to play me.

Eventually I began to improve. It's not really a game of much skill. I started to win. Then an extraordinary thing happened. When *I* lost I was expected to buy a round of drinks, but when the locals lost they said nothing. In the end I dropped a strong hint to my opponent, but he simply said, 'Oi didn't know we was playin' for gain. Oi don't hold with that sort of thing at all. 'Tes loike gamblin'.'

Later I spoke privately to the landlord and said I felt rather ashamed at having raised the matter, since farm labourers were not paid very well, and the landlord nearly exploded.

'Farm labourers?' he said. 'You must be joking. Most of them work on the industrial estate, and the bloke who wouldn't buy you a beer runs his own taxi business.'

Another great fallacy is that because a customer speaks with a local accent he is somehow wiser than a person who speaks the Queen's English, and has a store of native cunning. Like the man I met in a little Cornish pub while on a sailing cruise along the South Coast. He had a blue jersey and a Long John Silver accent so we asked him what he thought the weather would be like next day.

'Just you mark my words,' he said solemnly. 'You can bet your precious life it will start with a little mist about sunrise, but about eight-thirty it'll be raining hard and blowing a Force Six, mebbe even a Force Seven or more. Don't 'e go out tomorrow, my dears' (I apologize for the feeble effort to reproduce his accent).

We were immensely impressed, and my companion asked how he knew. Had he perhaps observed the colour of the sunset, the cloud formation, or the movements of the seagulls over the harbour?

'No,' he said. 'I listened to the six o'clock forecast on the television.'

We discovered later he was a lorry driver.

I am probably being a little hard on him, because his sort are infinitely preferable to those who have a little genuine folklore, and who force it upon innocent visitors as reliable wisdom, despite the fact that most pieces of local folklore were invented by people who thought the earth was flat. I once nearly wrecked a boat by heeding the advice of a local fisherman who swore it was bound to be calm weather next day because you always got good conditions when the cattle turned to face Rhubarb Wood (or some such rubbish). Next day, while thousands of cows solemnly turned to face Rhubarb Wood I was hanging on for life in the roughest sea I have ever known. I haven't been so scared since the TV licence-detector van stopped in our road. Give me the man who gets his forecast from the TV every time in preference to the public-bar bucolic who relies on the collected foolishness of the ages.

But perhaps you can't blame regular customers for behaving like something out of a British Tourist Board advert. The fact is, people expect them to behave like that. Visitors in particular, demand instant quaint old peasant, and if they don't find it they'll go to another pub which *can* supply it.

Just outside Stratford-on-Avon, on the Evesham road, there is a rather pleasant old inn. I was standing there one evening after a hard day in a television studio, when a group of American tourists came in and eyed me as if I was an ancient monument, nudging and pointing out to each other various peculiarities of my dress and person. Eventually one of the men said, 'Excuse me, but I expect you are busy with the lambing season?'

'No,' I replied. 'I have just come back from Birmingham.'

'You were seeking relaxation no doubt after a busy day with the sheep?'

'I have hardly ever seen a sheep in my life.'

'Of course not. This is cattle country, I expect.'

But country customers aren't the only ones to be the subject of fallacies. City pubs are always supposed to have a cheerful, wise, old philosopher in the corner seat. In reality, these cheerful philosophers in the corner seat are usually the biggest bores in the neighbourhood and one of their maddening habits is that they never, but never, pay any attention to what anybody else is saying.

I shall now quote almost verbatim the conversation I heard recently in the saloon bar of a pub in South Harrow between dear old Charlie, the corner-seat Moses, and a sad-looking chap who'd just walked in. Charlie spoke first:

'Hullo, hullo, hullo, who's Mr Misery then? What's the matter old son, lost half a crown and found sixpence? Heh, heh, heh.'

'No. I have just been sacked from my job after twenty years with the firm.'

'Look on the bright side, I always say.'

'My life's just a wreck.'

'Well, you've got to keep smiling, haven't you?'

'My wife's collapsed with shock.'

'Being happy's the only way to keep going, innit?'

'I feel so rotten, I wish I was dead.'

'That's more like it. Never say die.'

'I just said it you bloody fool.'

'All right, keep your hair on. Anyone'd think you'd had bad news.'

A further myth about the pub, is that it is the People's Parliament, the place where current affairs are thrashed out calmly yet vigorously in a spirit of give and take. This is of course rubbish, because the essence of a parliamentary debate is that you hear both sides, and you never hear both sides in a pub argument, because if customers find the others in the bar don't agree with their views they go to another pub where they do.

What passes for discussion in a pub is nothing of the sort, it's a mass orgy of moaning, with a sort of built-in crescendo so everybody caps what anyone else has said.

'I think they oughter do something about them there football hooligans.'

'Jail 'em, I say.'

'I'd flog 'em.'

'I'd flog 'em and then jail 'em.'

'I'd hang 'em.'

'I'd flog 'em and then hang 'em.'

'I'd give 'em a life sentence and then hang 'em at the end, just when they thought they was going to be released.'

'I'd hang their families as well. It's bred in the bone.'

Fortunately, however, there is one way of escape in an En-

glish pub, no matter how vile the conversation. As my old
Uncle Walter used to point out: 'The toilet is usually outside,
so that if you want to leave unobtrusively, you can go out there
and simply not come back.'

16 *When the Wheezes Won't Work*

My friend Askew claims to have won a golf cup by telling his opponent on the first tee that his dog had just died, but although grief-stricken he would carry on because the dog would have wished it. It's not often, however, that the pitiful wheezes of the Coarse Sportsman make headlines round the world. But they did in 1976 when the press resounded with the feats of Bobby Riggs, self-confessed woman-hater, who specialized in taking on top-class women tennis players twenty years or more his junior and beating them, helped by a campaign of psychological warfare that included being televised while eating raw meat. Poor Margaret Court was an early victim but Riggs got his come-uppance against Billie-Jean King in a match which attracted far more attention than a Wimbledon final. The *Sunday Times* asked me, as a student of Coarse Sport and its wheezes, to analyse the event:

You're old suddenly. The realization may come when you look into the shaving mirror and see large patches of white skin marching across the top of the scalp, where once hair proudly stood; or it may come when you wink at a pretty girl on a tube train and she shudders in repulsion.

For fifty-five-year-old Robert Larimore Riggs the moment came when he walked off court at Houston, Texas, after being beaten 6–4, 6–3, 6–3 by Wimbledon women's champion Billie-Jean King in the Battle of the Sexes. And the man who had sensationally beaten Margaret Court in a previous match found himself gloatingly described by the critics with such adjectives as 'bald, seedy and sagging'.

Riggs's defeat, however, was more than the physical losing of a tennis match by a pre-war Wimbledon champion to a woman twenty-six years younger than himself. The bitterest blow to the self-styled male chauvinist pig was his defeat in the psychological campaign before and during the match, an area in which he particularly prided himself on his superiority.

The idea of mind-warfare in sport is hardly new, of course, Muhammad Ali's been doing it for years. W. G. Grace used to draw the attention of young batsmen to something in the sky, so they were blinded by the sun and easy meat for his bowling. The immortal Stephen Potter described in *Gamesmanship* how he lost a tennis match because just before he served the first ball one of his opponents called out, 'Be careful, old chap, my partner is the Chilean Ambassador.' The far-from-immortal Michael Green was once dismissed for nought when playing cricket because the wicket-keeper muttered that the bowler had played for MCC, with the result that the simplest ball was treated as if it would explode. The bowler had NOT played for MCC.

Riggs's campaign, however, was far removed from such gentle tactics. He practised for the match by playing tennis with dogs chained to his ankles, with chairs scattered around court, while carrying a pail of water and on one occasion with a lion cub draped round his neck. He was photographed with a naked woman sprawling across his lap while he was gnawing a bone and dressed as Henry VIII.

His pre-match comments were equally unrestrained. 'When I get through with Billie she ought to go home and start raising a family. That's where she should be. That way women can't get out,' was one. Another was: 'When she plays me she'll see shots like she's never seen before.' Perhaps his most succinct statement was: 'I want to prove women are lousy. They stink. They don't belong on the same court as a man.' Good stuff from someone who's been divorced twice and who was taught to play tennis by a woman at the age of twelve.

Impressive though Riggs's stream of insults were, one can't help feeling that Mrs King won the Battle of the Lip. To all Riggs's taunts she made but one reply: 'There's no way you can psyche me out of winning. I have a cause.'

It was here Riggs made his big mistake. For in sporting psychological warfare insults aren't enough, at least, not unless they're backed up with overwhelming force. When the person insulted replied with dignified silence the insults have a way of rebounding. Instead of being rude and objectionable, Riggs might have achieved much more if he had played on Mrs King's womanly vanity by praising her lavishly and then touched a sympathetic nerve by announcing, just before the match began, *that he was suffering from an incurable disease*. How much more effective than insults to whisper, 'Good luck, Billie, and don't worry that this will be the last game before they amputate my leg.' No woman is going to beat a man who has just said that.

If Riggs insisted on using threats he should at least have realized that the subtly implied menace is far greater than a mere childish shout of, 'I'll get you.' An example Riggs might have followed is that of the rugby team I knew whose private psychopath used to talk to the opposition before a match and apologize in advance for one of their players.

'I thought it only fair to warn you about that big chap in the second row,' he would say. 'You can tell him because he keeps twitching and foaming and flaying his arms about uncontrollably. But he doesn't mean any harm. He can't help it. Since they put him on that course of drugs at the mental home he has improved tremendously. But it's probably better if you don't upset him. I think we all agreed with the judge that he was more to be pitied than blamed.'

But Riggs committed himself to strong-arm tactics and, having done so, he then allowed himself to be beaten at his own game, when Billie-Jean was carried into court on a pink litter, making Riggs's stunt of entering in a rickshaw appear pedestrian. When Riggs handed Mrs King a six-foot high lollipop with the charming remark, 'The largest sucker for the largest sucker,' she mentally wiped the floor with him by presenting him with a live pig.

After that, all she had to do was to prove that on court she was equally unmoved by Riggs's tennis tactics as by his insults. Riggs had beaten Margaret Court by playing what one of my ex-girl friends used to call Vicarage Tennis – lobs and spins calculated to goad any self-respecting woman into fury. The result was to drive poor Mrs Court into a frenzy (although her morale was already shattered by the fact that before the game her young son had thrown her tennis shoes down the lavatory and they hadn't dried). Mrs King simply refused to get rattled, and returned Riggs's lobs and spins with interest and sometimes in kind.

The lessons from this weird Lib–Lob contest are that it is unwise to use boasting and insults as weapons. They have a habit of bouncing back on the deliverer. It is far better to play on an opponent's finer feelings. And the strongest mental attack is useless unless you can put your racket where your mouth is.

Not that Riggs should worry. Despite his promise to jump off a bridge if he lost, he still collects 100 000 dollars. Presumably he'll laugh all the way to the river.

17

The Sound of the Master's Name

A moral recitation based on *The Old Violin* by Tex Ritter

An auctioneer was holding a sale.
The bidders crowded the hall.
There were watches, and diamonds and gold and gems
Till he came to Lot fifty four.

The bidders laughed as he held aloft
Two battered old rugby boots.
'How much am I bid for this interesting lot?'
And a voice cried, 'Twopence, old fruit.'

'Any advance on twopence?' he cried,
But the bidders started to bawl.
'Don't hold up the sale with this rubbish, old chap,
You're wasting the time of us all.'

Then suddenly the people fell back
And an old man pushed through as they stared
'Let me look at them boots – yes, I know them well,
They were Barry John's favourite pair.

'It was six years ago, he wore them that day.
When he beat the All Blacks on his own.
And he gave them away to my wife don't you see
For our grandson to wear as his own.

'But hard times came on us, our money ran out
I gambled away all our cash.

And I sobbed as I drank every glass

I took out Barry's boots and I sold 'em for drink –
And I sobbed as I drank every glass.

'And now I am dying and soon I'll be gone
To the Great Referee in the Sky
But give me them boots, let me just put 'em on –
Let me wear them once more ere I die.'

When the old man had finished there wasn't a sound
From the hard-faced men in the hall.
Till the auctioneer banged his hammer and cried,
'Let's start off the bidding once more.'

'A hundred, two hundred,' the bidders cried.
The price rose by leaps and by bounds.
Those rich men fought to possess the boots –
They were sold for six hundred pounds.

The Moral is this, as we pass through Life
On our way to the Last Great Game.
That the magic which always turns lead into gold
Is the Sound of the Master's Name.

18 Bedroom Secret Turns Rabbit into Tiger

Golfers are easy meat for miracle cures and aids to better play, ranging from apparatus to warming golf balls to springs for exercising vital hand muscles. Coarse Golfers are particularly susceptible, because lacking any natural ability they have to believe that success can be bought over the counter, which accounts for the incredible industry which has sprung up in providing golfing aids, including 'elasticated driving underwear'. Honestly, I saw some advertised. They claimed it improved your stance. A friend bought some, put it on backwards, and injured himself on the first tee. In the following two pieces, the *Sunday Times* had commissioned me to test out the latest advertised short cuts to golf success.

The advertisement was headed: 'I was a 116 golfer.' Underneath it said: 'Within ten days I got down to 74!'

It went on: 'My name is Allan Sadler. I'm fifty-five years old, had dozens of lessons, own sixty four books on the game and hit thousands of balls on the range. The result? 116. I hated golf !'

Mr Sadler seemed a man after my own heart. I am forty nine years old. I own six books on the game and I don't take any lessons but the result is often 116 or more. I not only hate golf but I hate people like Mr Sadler who keep telling me what I am doing wrong.

Yet Mr Sadler certainly seemed to have discovered the secret. It came to him, he revealed in his advertisement, like many of the greatest inventions, in a flash of intuition, of understanding 'one dark morning'.

'I got up,' said Mr Sadler somewhat mysteriously, 'tested it in front of the mirror – and waited for dawn. *I knew I had it!*'

On the assumption that Mr Sadler was, in fact, talking about the secret of golf and not about something else, I accepted his invitation to send £2.50 to an address in Surrey and receive details of the 'magic move' by which his scores went from 116 to 74 in ten days. Even his friends' handicaps went down as well, he claimed, although I would have preferred something that improved my own game and ruined that of my friends.

Not long afterwards a slim, modest volume, produced with the aid of a typewriter on orange paper arrived, and I learned the secret of the magic move.

Before revealing it, however, Mr Sadler treats the reader to the story of his unhappy golfing life. This appears to have been spent entirely in the hands of maniacal professionals who told him to imagine he was standing in a barrel, swinging with a plate of glass hanging from his neck; or having his hips pulled round by giant rubber band. The result? 116. He once lost a dozen balls in 18 holes. He topped, drooped, shanked and wiffed (whatever that means).

Then came that sudden inspiration, the magic move which was to turn Mr Sadler from a rabbit to a tiger in ten days. It was simply: *drop the left chest on the backswing and raise it on the downswing.*

'Every other move of your body,' writes Mr Sadler, 'after lowering and raising your left chest, is secondary! ... Left chest down! Left chest up! And that is it!'

For the rest of the book Mr Sadler expands on his theme, which he claims can even be adapted to putting. 'When you have a good line, taking into account all factors such as slope, grain, etc., drop your left chest, pause and then raise the left chest. There is no separate hand, wrist or arm movement. The putting swing is just like a full swing.'

Armed with Mr Sadler's advice, I set out to test it with my friend (handicap 12). I stood on the first tee and solemnly tried to drop my right chest (I am left-handed). I may say it is not easy to drop half your chest. It seems attached to the other half.

'Are you in pain?' asked my partner.

'Jealous idiot,' I thought.

Having at last succeeded in lowering it, I raised my right chest and smote. Three shots later I was still on the tee. So was the ball. There was no sign of the rapid progression from 116 experienced by Mr Sadler. After three strokes I abandoned the magic move (which had cost me 83½p per shot) and went back to the old style. Actually it wasn't a bad round. I'd have broken 100 if it hadn't been for the three air shots on the tee, plus a hole where I five-putted from three feet while trying to raise and lower the chest.

Yet somehow I felt it might be all *my* fault. If it worked for Mr Sadler, why not me? Glancing through the book again I saw that the distributors listed other literary guides to success. They advertised companion volumes on training dogs, success at tennis (also secured in ten days, thanks to 'The Missile Swing'), how to get a better job, and a book dealing with male sexual problems.

Then came the realization. Dear Mr Sadler, did I get the wrong book? Did they send the sex book by mistake? Perhaps the advice given was meant to be hints on how to cure impotence? After all, did not Mr Sadler significantly say the idea came to him in the bedroom? Note the phraseology: 'I got up, tested it in front of a mirror ... I knew I had it!'

Meanwhile enquirers after the sex volume may have received the golf book, and all over the country desperate husbands could be saying: 'But darling, the book quite definitely said I was to stand with my feet eighteen inches apart, lean forward and swing from the hips. . . .'

Mr Sadler, you may have started something bigger than you think. But just answer this one question: What's the sexual equivalent of going from 116 to 74 in ten days?

19 At Last - I've Got Golf Taped

I stood in the big bunker to the left of the fifth green at Royal Mid-Surrey, Richmond. The calm, slightly lilting Welsh voice of Dai Rees spoke from just behind me.

'Too many golfers are frightened of bunkers ... it's the awful power of negative thinking,' he said quietly. I grunted agreement. Quite right. There were too many cowards in golf today. Scared of a little sand.

'A bunker shot is the one shot you can buy in the pro's shop,' went on Dai encouragingly. 'Get a good sand wedge.' I had got a good sand wedge. And I had bought it in the pro's shop.

I started the backswing, remembering Dai's earlier words on the first tee, that I should try to think of the rim of a cartwheel and take my arm back with the clubhead. As I swung down I could hear Dai telling me 'with a good sand iron any golfer, man or woman, can get out of a bunker if they select a spot behind the ball, hit the sand, follow through and don't blast. . . .'

I smote. Sand flew in all directions and over in the near-by Royal Botanical Gardens at Kew, a small, white speck was seen to disappear through the trees. Dai was still talking. I took the newly-purchased sand wedge (bought at the pro's shop), adjusted my stance in the way he recommended, and struck again. This time it was a perfect shot. The tape recorder went spinning out of the bunker and the droning voice stopped with a terrified squawk.

Perhaps it was really my fault, not Dai's. After all, Times Cassettes, who had produced the instructional tape, don't

This time it was a perfect shot

actually recommend that you play it on the course, except in the practice area. But if it's not designed for advice during a round it's difficult to see what a tape can do that a book can't. After all, quite a lot of golfers can read, and some can write their names as well.

Of course, there's nothing new about coaching gadgets being taken along. In the past they've ranged from a sort of plaster cast on the neck to keep the head still to inflatable collars for keeping the left elbow straight when driving. Plenty of players have adopted little things to remind them to do right as they play.

Not everyone goes as far as the man I once met who had pasted a whole list of wrinkles on a board which he hung from his trolley, so that when he got into deep rough, for instance, he would look up the suitable section and then open the club-face or whatever was appropriate. Very useful were those tips, and I was glad to borrow them. And few players would be as conscientious as a friend who painted the second knuckle of his right hand blue ('If I can see a spot of blue when I grip the club, then I know I'm turning my hand over').

But the dangerous thing about a tape is its human quality. A book is inanimate, and at least one can throw it away or tear it up, but the calm voice of a tape droning away as you muff a shot is an open invitation to assault. Especially when you do everything it says, and still put the ball out of bounds.

It is all too reminiscent of the partner who talks during one's backswing, the sort of human filth who suddenly steps forward as you address the ball and remarks, 'Look old man, I don't want to interrupt your stroke, but do you know you are holding the club all wrong?'

Having said all that, it must be stated that the advice given, in the form of a conversation between our own golf correspondent Dudley Doust and Dai himself, is commendably down-to-earth and practical as Dai takes the listener on an imaginary hole from tee to green.

'Golf is a right-handed game for right-handers, and a left-handed game for left-handers,' asserts Dai, brushing aside all that nonsense about the left hand doing the work. He advocates using lofted clubs wherever possible, even to the extent of taking a five or six wood off the fairway, and prefers the pitch-and-run to the wedge shot.

All good solid stuff for the middle-handicap man, although I am not sure about his forthright statement, 'Unless your swing is a disaster, don't change it.'

Not even if it's *square*, like mine?

One feels, though, that the tape might have been improved with better direction. There are rather a lot of contrived situations, with Dudley made to say remarks like, 'OK Dai, I'll try it your way with a two wood,' followed by a loud swish. There's also some rather pointless music which sounds like *The Dance of the Shankers*, but which may be something else. This, however, is balanced by the professionalism of Harry Carpenter's summaries.

Altogether, a two-edged production. Played quietly at home it must improve your golf. Played on the course it could wreck it. Played in your car, as recommended by the producers, it might kill you. An ideal Christmas gift for someone you hate.

20 *The Great Grub Street Stakes*

It would never have done for Lunchtime O'Booze, legendary media man of *Private Eye* fame. Here are nearly fifty Fleet Street journalists standing around in running kit on a chilly day at Crystal Palace and they are going to race 1.39 miles round the outer perimeter road; they are all sober; they are doing it for charity and, I kid you not old man, they aren't even putting it on their expenses.

Yes, the Great Grub Street Stakes turned out to be far removed from the jocular contest between two teams of paunchy inebriates which one might have expected. Like one of those friendly cricket matches which suddenly turn nasty when a player gets hit on the head, the whole thing became almost distressingly serious, despite its origins, which lay in a drunken challenge from John Lovesey, *Sunday Times* Sports Editor, to freelance athletics writer John Goodbody, which materialized last week with the *Sunday Times* taking on the rest of Fleet Street in a team race.

Fortunately for the peace of the sports room, the *Sunday Times* won, which is not surprising, as they entered more four-man teams than anybody else. Second was the *Evening News*, and third the *Guardian*. Tenth and last was also the *Sunday Times*, however – the 'C' team.

Alas, two men are missing from the *Sunday Times* squad – the Editor and myself. I had actually gone into training when after a sprint across Ealing Common I experienced a psychic revelation. As I knelt gasping for breath, lights flashed across my eyes and I distinctly saw my own obituary in *The Times*.

'SCOOP' GREEN COLLAPSES IN RACE
EXPENSES SHEET CLUTCHED IN HAND
DEATH RATTLE HEARD AT UPMINSTER
PRESIDENT OF RUGBY UNION GRIEF-STRICKEN

You don't ignore a warning like that. I walked home and rang up to say I'd got 'flu. 'Flu had also struck Harold Evans, the editor, which is a pity because I had been looking forward to writing how kind, wise and generous he is.

Chris Brasher* is also absent. It is rumoured he withdrew because they wouldn't let him tie his ankles together with barbed wire to make it more difficult.

However, there are still plenty of well-known names around as Jim Fox, the Olympic gold medallist, and others from the Modern Pentathlon Association, marshal the shivering runners.

Among them is Robin Marlar, a trifle portlier than when he played for Sussex, giving instructions about how he is to be revived in case of collapse or, failing that, how his remains are to be disposed of. To cheer him up I recall the last time I dropped out of a race. It was an army brigade cross-country in the bitter German winter of 1947, and the soldier who took my place was carried in with a frostbitten penis. He never forgave me.

Robin Marlar goes pale and moves away, clutching his loins, but it is too late to withdraw for they are off, on a time handicap based on age and the first away is the oldest, fifty-year-old Alan Hitchings, features editor of the *People*. And 1.39 miles and 7.45 minutes later he is first back, heading the field by fifty yards and looking fresh.

Journalists are the worst people in the world to interview and getting a good quote from the runners is difficult. Alan Hitchings, for instance, is modest to the point of reticence, strange for a man who spends his life writing headlines like: WHY DON'T THEY REVEAL THE TRUTH? But all he will say is, 'Now that I've reached fifty, I don't do any serious running. Just the odd marathon.'

It turns out he is one of a group of journalists in the race

---

*That's the second crack about Chris Brasher in this book. Sorry.

'I don't do any serious running. Just the odd marathon'

who took part in the Barnsley marathon, his time being 2.54. Among the others are thirty-five-year-old Colin Henderson, also of the *People*, who got up at 4 a.m. to drive to Barnsley, ran twenty-six miles and drove back for his evening shift. The group can be seen every lunchtime maniacally running a dozen miles or so across the Thames bridges and back.

But it's not only the serious runners who are making their mark. True, former Cambridge Blue John Bryant (*Daily Mail*), another of the Barnsley gang, is second, but there's some heroic work further back. *Guardian* sports writer John Rodda, who is forty-seven, comes in twelfth literally foaming at the mouth.

I look round desperately for someone else to give him the kiss of life and ask: 'How did it go, John?'

'Glug,' he replies as he totters past grey-faced to collapse over a chair.

And so it goes on. John Hopkins, *Sunday Times* rugby correspondent, arrives, viciously shouldering past two others at the finish in a manner that would earn a penalty in a Twickenham line-out. First woman home is Jill Linscott, of the *Guardian*, thirty-first overall, and second girl is our own Chris Oram, her generous bosom covered with a T-shirt saying: 'I suffered for the *Sunday Times*'. Thirty-ninth is Kevin Murphy, of the *Evening Standard*, better known for having swum the Channel both ways twice, and for winning this year's Sydney Harbour race. 'Give me the Channel any time,' he grunts.

Last two are charming lassies from the *Morning Star*, Pat Smith and Sheila Gray, who provide the most intriguing quote: 'Neither of us have ever done it before but we quite enjoyed it.'

But the drama is not over. Hardly has the last competitor tottered away than a lonely, pale determined figure is seen running on to the deserted track. It is our Editor, Harold Evans (forty-nine), who has decided to run against the clock, despite illness. And I would like to take this opportunity of saying how wise, generous and kind this man is. He's also quite a nifty runner, for he turns in 9.15 which would have put him twelfth, just behind forty-five-year-old Neil Allen, of the *Evening News*.

And so to the bar (after all, it *is* a Fleet Street occasion) where well deserved euphoria abounds. As John Bryant says, 'The old cry is athletics from the coaches to the critics is, why don't you do it yourself if you're so clever? I reckon today shows our six best Fleet Street men could beat the six best coaches any time.'

When the results are announced it is revealed that Debenhams, who are sponsoring the event, will be handing £270 to the British Paraplegic Sports Society, based on £10 for everyone who beat ten minutes and £1 for the others. Plans are laid for an even more ambitious race along the Embankment next year.

But the spirit of Fleet Street still remains, despite the unjournalistic physical activity. 'The free drinks supplied by Debenhams are finished, ladies and gentlemen,' announces the barman. Within five minutes the place is empty.

21 *A Trip down Memory Drain*

I was talking to a friend the other week, and we spent an evening over the pints discussing old times, mostly rugger with a bit of golf and womanizing thrown in, and at the end of the evening my friend remarked, 'Do you know, we've been talking all night about when we played together, and we haven't remembered one good thing that happened to us. We must have enjoyed *some* of the games surely?' And he was right, of course. All our reminiscences had been, not about the time when we beat half-a-dozen men to score the winning try, but about such occasions as when the car broke down and we got to Oxford on hired bicycles, only to lose 38–0, being completely exhausted before the wretched match even began.

That, however, is typical of a Coarse Sportsman's most memorable experiences. The one advantage this gives him is that he doesn't usually have any tragedies to recall, unless one regards failing to arrive in time for the Third XV as a tragedy. He is spared the lifelong guilt of some poor soul who loses a chance of the Triple Crown for his country with a poor penalty kick at goal; neither does he have to recall the misery of say, a hostile press campaign. Much more likely his memories will be of dreadful humiliations, like the corporal who was playing in goal for my troop in the regimental soccer cup. He was attacked by a cloud of wasps and had to flee from the field, leaving an empty goalmouth through which the ball was duly dribbled.

It is, incidentally, typical of coarse sport, that nobody paid any attention to his excuse. If he had been a famous goal-keeper, they'd have all said, 'Bad show, these wretched wasps should be dealt with,' and the groundsman would have been blamed for not blocking up their nest, but no Coarse Sportsman receives any sympathy in disaster. The unhappy corporal was promptly marked down by the officers as emotionally unstable.

Looking back for my most sensational sporting memory, I find several happenings jostling each other for attention. In the end I've decided my greatest moment was when I ensured victory for my rugby team by tackling the referee. It was one of those matches in which we had only eleven men to our opponents' fifteen, but with tremendous ingenuity and courage we determined to give them a good game, and by using such tactics as rushing around waving our arms madly in all directions to make it look as if there were more of us than there were, we actually got into the lead. Five minutes from time, however, the opposition broke away and a try seemed certain. But before they crossed the line I smartly tackled the referee round the knees from behind and as soon as he'd got up and found his glasses he promptly blew for a scrummage.

One of my most terrible experiences took place off the field of play, at a rugby dinner. It was given by an old boys' club on the Kent coast. I decided to deliver my standard speech which had been knocking 'em under the tables at about thirty other functions that season, and I didn't see why it shouldn't do the same thing on this occasion.

Now this speech was what I would call a robust talk. Not one for the squeamish, the faint-hearted, or the puritanical, but one for the lads. It sounded better spoken than it looked written down and was more impressive if the listeners were drunk rather than sober. The speech notes read rather like a medical treatise:

BLIND PROSTITUTE

MAN WITH NO ARMS

DOCTOR WHO PRESCRIBED ASPIRIN IN MISTAKE FOR PILL

WELSH GIRL AND SCOTTISH SEX MANIAC

IRISHMAN WHO HAD TWO

MAN WHO TRIED TO HAVE IT OFF IN BALLOON

Unfortunately I arrived late – largely due to the inaccurate route details supplied – so I had little chance to survey my audience before I was thrust into the firing line, as one might say. However, I was greeted with generous applause, which convinced me that once again I was going to knock them cold as I replied to the toast of the guests.

'Gentlemen,' I began, with the well modulated sneer of the professional egotist who knows he's got his audience on toast. 'I should like to start off by paying you all a great tribute.' (*Pause to make the follow-up more effective.*) I should like to begin by saying that you remind me of a load of blind prostitutes. (*Slight pause before pay-off.*) And what I always say about blind prostitutes is that you've got to hand it to them.'

I waited. I usually had to do so at this point to allow the laughter to subside. But this time there was complete silence, except for some embarrassed coughing.

I tried again.

'No, I didn't mean that seriously, chaps, ha, ha, ha. I really wanted to tell you about the woman who ran a brothel and there was a long ring on the doorbell and she went downstairs and there stood a man with no arms, and she said, "What are you doing here, you've got no arms, you're no use here," and he said, "Well I rang the bell all right, didn't I?" '

When I had told that story at Portsmouth RFC they had fallen off their chairs with mirth and the chairman choked with laughter so much so they had to beat him on the back. On this occasion, to say it was not well received would be an under-statement. It fell like a wet flannel on the floor. In fact my listeners did not even appear to be looking at me – they were staring at someone further along the top table.

I looked at my 'notes'. Somewhere near the end was a joke that was almost clean (provided you cut out the swear words). I hastily rattled it off, received precisely one laugh in response, and sat down in total silence.

The club chairman rose.

'Gentlemen, our President will now address us.' The President stood up, and I saw why everyone had been looking at him. He had a clerical collar with the purple stock of a bishop. He was also six foot four and the most red-faced, formidable man I have ever seen in my life. And he was not smiling. 'Oh Lord,' he boomed in a voice that might have been in Southend, and probably was. 'Grant that we may be worthy of this great game of rugby union not only on the field but in our everyday lives, and that as we play cleanly so may we *live cleanly, and talk cleanly and think cleanly.*' I think there was some more but I was out of the room before he got any further.

I have had so many bad moments at golf it is difficult to pick out any particular one. There was the time I hit the horse of a Wimbledon Common Ranger and he pursued me through the woods on his injured steed; the time I kicked the sand in a bunker in a rage and sprained my ankle; or the occasion when I was actually mistaken for a caddy at Walton Heath. This was particularly embarrassing because I was playing with the golf correspondent of the *Sunday Times*, who bitterly resented the disgrace. 'Damned if I'll ever play with a shabby b—— like you again,' he muttered grimly. On the whole, however, I believe my worst moment was when I lost my grip on the club on the first tee and it soared into the car park, where it shattered the windscreen of a Mercedes.

Cricket, too, has provided its fair share of despair, including a ghastly moral dilemma. That happened when I was umpiring for my side. Now the odd thing about player–umpires is that they are expected to be impartial. Non-playing umpires, those elderly malcontents employed by the same side week after week, are usually *expected* to be biassed in favour of their own team, but the tradition is that *players* when standing play fair, perhaps because they know they'll get a bumper round the ears if they don't, when it's their turn to bat. But I have to confess to breaking this tradition once. I not only deliberately gave one of my own side Not Out when he was plainly and fairly dismissed, but I did it several times running.

The batsman was dear old Alec. Alec was one of the keenest members of the side. He was also the team clown and sometimes he'd put on dark glasses to bat and grope his way to the wicket and then ask the umpire in his white coat for two ice creams and that sort of thing. The only trouble was that Alec was also the complete all-rounder. He could neither bat, bowl nor field. This didn't really matter, since we were a touring side out for the beer and results hardly counted, but there came a match when it did matter a lot to Alec. He was being moved by his firm to another part of the country and he came to this last match with the realization he had never scored a single run against our opponents in seven years.

'I should like to think I'd got just one run against 'em,' he told the skipper, who promoted him to number eight to give him a chance. I was umpiring when Alec came out to bat. It was obvious from the way he groped blindly forward, peering from behind his pebble glasses, that he was not going to last. The first ball shaved the stumps, he never saw the second and the third bowled him. Alec started to walk sadly back when I did the unspeakable thing. 'No ball,' I shouted firmly. The bowler looked at me as if I was insane so I added, 'I couldn't call before as I had a gnat in my throat.' Alec returned to the wicket while all the fielders glared at me savagely, and the bowler sent down a snorter which had him plumb l.b.w. 'I'm sorry,' I said in reply to his bellowed appeal, 'but you keep running across my line of vision. I can't possibly give an l.b.w.' I don't like to recall the next couple of minutes during which I saved Alec on three more occasions, twice with imaginary no balls. Finally, they ran two on a ball which hit his leg, I refused to signal leg-bye, so Alec got his runs, and next ball I gave him out l.b.w. although the ball never hit his pads. Even the fielders were dumbfounded.

I walked in with the feeling of a man who has done his duty, but if I expected any gratitude from Alec I was mistaken.

'That was a very strange decision when you gave me out,' he said stiffly. 'It was a great pity, because I was just getting my eye in.'

Although I describe that story as a moral dilemma, I don't really believe in attributing high moral virtues to sport. Cricket suffers a lot from that and I still remember this gem from a Victorian novel: 'Jack lowered the horsewhip. "I'll give you one more chance," he said sternly. "A man who batted first wicket down for Middlesex can't be bad all the way through." '

As one who found in later life that many cricketers at my level at any rate, were merely second-rate cheats (they weren't even good at cheating, let alone cricket), I was not entirely surprised to find that similar virtues attributed to yachtsmen ('He must be OK if he can handle a forty-foot sloop in a Force

Seven') were equally phoney. My own sailing experience is that if you want to meet a thorough-going four-star lout then you should meet the owner of a large yacht, and the larger the yacht the loutier the owner will be.

My most memorable sailing experience, for instance, was not clawing off a lee shore in a gale but took place in a marina on the South Coast. We were just sitting down to dinner when all the light was blocked out by a large shape approaching and a bowsprit silently entered the cabin through an open porthole and pinned our skipper to the side of the cabin.

'I'm sorry,' came a cheerful voice from outside, with masterly understatement, 'I couldn't get reverse.'

Our skipper said nothing (partly because you can't speak very well with a bowsprit in your chest). But when he recovered he took out a saw from the tool locker and without saying a word started to saw off the offending sprit. He was halfway through before they managed to withdraw. So much for the moral virtues of sailing.

My last horrid memory is The Strange Case of the Curry Sandwiches. It was more years ago than I care to remember and I was playing cricket in Birmingham. Those were the days when immigrants were a novelty; but we had an Indian in our side, a cheerful chap of about thirty-five who spent his time in a bed-sitter studying for endless examinations and cooking curry. He was the only man I know who ate curry for breakfast, lunch, tea, dinner and supper. One Saturday we met for a beer at lunch-time before the game and he kindly invited me to share his packet of curry sandwiches. I had never had curry sandwiches before, but I must say they were delicious apart from a slight tendency to shrivel up the tongue.

About seven that evening I was fielding and I was just about to cross the pitch at the end of an over when a terrible spasm seized me and my insides turned to water, as if a curry sandwich (for instance) had disagreed with me. I stopped and remained rooted to the spot. Experience of this sort of thing had taught me that the slightest move could prove fatal.

The fact that I hadn't crossed over remained unnoticed. In that class of cricket nobody bothers if mid-on is thirty yards out of position. I remained nailed to the ground at what would be called silly square leg if anyone was daft enough to field four feet from the bat.

I began to call for help, but our slowest bowler was already beginning the three shambling steps he called his run. I watched horrified as he sent down his standard ball, a gentle full toss just outside the leg stump. A look of glee spread over the batsman's face as he prepared to swing it to leg and if death did not exactly stare me in the face it was glancing in my direction quite a bit. I covered my face with my hands turned away and waited for the blow. Nothing happened. There was much shouting and when I looked up the batsmen were running while the ball lay stationary between my feet. A run out would have been certain but for the fact I couldn't bend down to pick it up. In the end they ran three before I could indicate, chiefly by signs, that I could not bend to pick up the ball.

22 Games People Play with Olympics

Nothing could be further from the world of Coarse Sport than the Olympic Games with their ballyhoo, hysteria, politics and corruption. In 1980 the next lot open in Moscow. But the ripples of the 1976 Games went on for a long time as I found when I visited Montreal after the Games that year.

If anyone thinks the Olympic Games are over as far as Montreal is concerned, they'd be wrong. Firstly, they're still talking about them, secondly they're still paying for them, and thirdly they haven't even finished the stadium yet. When I was there last week, workmen were busy on the vast 500-foot tower which will eventually contain an indoor sports complex and restaurant and support a removable plastic roof. They hope to finish it next year. Or by the Moscow Olympics anyway.

Meanwhile the sacred turf inside the track where Viren strode majestically while David Coleman had hysterics all over his microphone, has been torn up and concreted over for artificial grass on which the Allouettes, Montreal's gridiron football team, will play.

The big question, of course, remains: who is going to pay for it all? Are Montreal and the Province of Quebec to be mortgaged forever to a colossal white elephant? The story of how everyone jumped on the bandwaggon as costs escalated from $120 million to over $1000 million until Montreal had to relinquish control, is now history. Less well known is that interest on the deficit of $750 million is a staggering £116 000 *a day*, and daily running costs of the stadium complex are said to be $50 000 on top of that.

The sale of souvenirs and coins, guided tours (300 000 so far at $2.50 each) and a lottery will help towards paying off the deficit, but unless the Olympics are to be a permanent tax burden, the stadium must pay its way by letting. Here the outlook is not hopeful. The 10 000-seat velodrome, built at a cost of one million dollars for each registered track cyclist in the country – all fifty of them – only attracted 300 a day for the recent national championships. Bobby Riggs got 2000 people to see him beat Andree Martin at Lib–Lob tennis.

In the main stadium the Allouettes, for their opening game, have sold all 72 000 tickets. At an average of $10 a ticket, this would mean $72 000 for the Olympic Installation Board, who are reputed to be demanding 10 per cent. But even this is much less than the daily operating costs and interest combined. And the Allouettes only have half a dozen home games each season.

Montreal's top baseball side, the Expos, will also use the stadium, but unfortunately they are currently baseball's equivalent of Accrington Stanley. They will be pleased to move from Jarry Park, where visitors are inclined to ask when they drive the cows on the field, but gates are as low as 4000, and with admission prices cheaper than those for football, they can hardly provide the answer.

'There is no way the stadium can pay,' says local newspaper columnist Alan Richman, 'unless you can book the Rolling Stones every night.'

It is typical of the fog which has surrounded the whole thing that when I tried to talk to Michel Guay, the new head of the OIB, about the stadium's letting potential, he referred me to Jean Riendeau, OIB's Head of Communications, who also declined to see me, but suggested I contacted Mr Guay.

So I sought the fountain-head, Jean Drapeau, mayor for nearly twenty years, and hero, pharaoh, *gauleiter*, ruin or saviour of Montreal according to opinion. Drapeau, small, sixty, a bundle of energy, is one of the last of the great North American city bosses, somewhat in the tradition of Mayor Daley of Chicago, or La Guardia of New York. He built the

Metro, the Expo '67, he got the Games, and is now rumoured to be bidding for the UN headquarters to be moved to Montreal.

Whatever one may say about him – and his opponents call him everything from a snake-oil salesman to a Mussolini – his striking personality cannot be denied. Upon my modestly asking what he was going to do about the $200 million which the OIB has charged the city as its share of the financial carnage, he fixed me with a far-from-beady eye and said firmly: 'Tell them I shall not pay one goddam cent.'

I reminded him that he originally said the Games would be self-financing. How did he reconcile that with the fact that the Province of Quebec had levied a cigarette tax to help pay for them? He replied with sweeping financial judgement of breathtaking simplicity which would have baffled Keynes himself.

'Just as I said, they are self-financing. What is three cents on a packet of cigarettes but self-financing? If I'd had my way I'd have taxed booze too. If you want to support the Games, you smoke. If you don't want to pay the tax, you don't smoke. Self-financing.'

He denied allegations that many civic improvements, housing, transport and sewage have been delayed because of the Games (11 000 Montreal houses have no bathrooms), and blamed instead inflation, the money market and Government interference. 'Not one housing project has been held up,' he maintained.

Was it all worthwhile in view of the hassle?

'Of course,' he said. 'The most important part of the Games comes afterwards. They wouldn't be worth it as a mere sporting show, but it's the effect they have. We had no amateur sport in Canada to speak of before the Games. Now millions have participated in it through watching the Games. Already the kids are demanding more facilities. We were an underprivileged nation as far as amateur sport went before, now all that is changed.

'There is tremendous pride here in what we have achieved. Faced with our difficulties, any other city would have given up.'

Well, the people of Montreal certainly keep voting for Drapeau's Civic Party, and for his efforts to drag Montreal kicking and screaming into the Big League. 'He's changed us from a village to an international city,' said a girl telephone employee. 'Even the food's changed. He's put us on the map.'

The shoeshine man was less enthusiastic. 'Terrible,' he wailed. 'Those Games were just terrible. They've sowed the seeds of World War Three right here in Montreal. Well, if it comes, I'm going straight back to live with my married daughter in New Brunswick.'

But a truck driver said: 'He's clever, that Drapeau. He gets things for Montreal, and persuades the rest of Canada to pay for them.'

One can't really judge Montreal by the standards of an English urban council. It is the second largest French-speaking city in the world, an international crossroads situated in a province which contains a million lakes (one for every six people), and where hotels put up notices: 'Please do not moor your sea-plane here, but in the space provided.'

Montreal, bustling with new-found confidence, needs a leader to channel its energies. If Mayor Drapeau did not exist they would have to invent him. And if the Olympics hadn't existed they would have invented *them*.

23 The Art of Coarse Rowing

The Egyptian Government used to have the pleasant habit, a year or two back, of inviting the universities of Yale, Harvard, Oxford and Cambridge to row against each other on the Nile, together with local crews. There were two races, one upstream at Luxor, the ancient city of Thebes, burial place of the Pharoahs, and a second race in Cairo. The series continued for some years until it became a casualty of the Israel–Egypt conflict. I think it can be said that this spectacular river occasion was one of the few times that Coarse Sport – in this case Rowing – has reached international level.

It was all rather different from Putney Bridge. True, there were Oxford and Cambridge waiting nervously at the stakeboats but then, this was the Nile at Luxor and the event was the first of the two races which made up last week's international Nile rowing festival.

The Luxor end of the contest can claim to be the world's oldest boat race, going back more than 5000 years to the time when the citizens of Thebes competed for the honour of rowing the effigy of the god Amun in a religious river procession.

It is also a highly unusual race. One year a team ran into a dead camel floating in the river, while last time Oxford mistook a fanfare from the temple ruins as the finishing signal and stopped rowing 100 yards too soon.

It must also be the only boat race in the world where the press launch has to travel in front of the rowers, because it can't keep up with them. I say launch, but in fact it was an ancient and enormous two-decker which looked as if it once belonged to Sanders of the River.

This contraption was steered from the bows by a genial

lunatic in an old nightshirt who kept sounding on his hooter the international signal for, 'I am on fire and have dangerous cargo on board.' This may have been no coincidence; his sister-craft ran aground early on with 500 gibbering passengers.

It was difficult to see the start of the 2 000-metre race because our captain took up his position by the finishing-post. But it was later reported that the man holding Oxford to the stake-boat let go and they shot downstream as the starter cleared his throat. The other five crews all protested but nobody took any notice and they set off in hot pursuit.

As the boats approached, however, it could be seen that Harvard had gained the lead, striking a nifty 38 opposite Abdul's souvenir stall, the Luxor equivalent of Harrods' warehouse. Behind them Oxford and Cambridge were engaged in a grim struggle, with Cambridge just holding a lead of a canvas, despite the handicap of having seven strokes in their crew.

Unfortunately, for reasons best known to our babbling captain, the press boat chose this moment to turn round in circles. I found myself staring at an old peasant eating an onion on the other bank.

One hundred guests on the upper deck promptly rushed to the other rail and we took a list of 45 degrees. It was like the last moment of the *Titanic*. The situation was saved only by the bravery of Reuter's correspondent, who manhandled the fattest passengers back to our side.

By the time the race came back into view, Harvard were shooting past the winning-post, followed by Cambridge, Oxford, the Egyptians and Yale. The winning time was given as 5 min. 17 sec. which according to the *Egyptian Gazette* was three minutes faster than last year. The sensational improvement was, however, because someone forgot to stop their watch the previous time.

The more serious leg of the festival was rowed three days later at Cairo, and some of the Cambridge crew took some unusual training by having a race as to who could climb a pyramid the fastest, and at night too.

The expedition was suggested by *The Times* reporter. Apparently he had asked *The Times* library for some books to help a traveller in Egypt and all they could produce was a 1905 copy of Baedeker. Now Baedeker is quite explicit about pyramid climbing. In a section somewhat ambiguously entitled 'How to Have Intercourse with Orientals,' the traveller is urged to select two 'of the importunate Bedouin' to pull him up by his hands. It adds: 'The traveller may be assisted by a third (no extra payment) who pushes from behind.'

Cambridge ran up by themselves, accompanied by the gallant *Times* correspondent, who was promptly prostrated for twenty-four hours. Whether it affected Cambridge equally is uncertain, but they were noticeably sluggish in the next day's race, being well beated for third place by Oxford. Once again Harvard won, but this time an Egyptian team made a strong challenge and came second by half a length.

Despite the holiday atmosphere the festival is more competitive than might be thought. Yale were bitterly disappointed by their failures, while Oxford were equally keen to beat Cambridge even if only on the Nile. Not that either crew was representative. Cambridge were mostly men who had gone down and Oxford had perhaps four contenders for the Boat Race.

But the festival has started to become famous. Certainly press coverage was worthy of in international event with nearly a dozen reporters from Britain and the US present. None were rowing correspondents though, and one US paper sent its gardening expert. There was an Evelyn Waugh flavour about the press corps which suggested they had received telegrams like: 'Inform Smith unreport flower show, proceed Thebes-wise speediest.'

Harvard brought their own Director of Sports Information, who found communications from Luxor difficult. He was seen tottering white-faced into the hotel lobby and complaining bitterly, 'Gee, that goddam clerk wanted to charge me $138 to cable the States that I'd arrived.'

The festival is over but the memories linger on. Dearest of all, I shall long cherish the sight of the Yale crew hastily rowing back to the boathouse because one of their number had suddenly been smitten by the complaint we came to call The Curse of the Pharaohs.

Cambridge ran up by themselves

24 *An Ode on the Battle of Twickenham*

Surprisingly, there's hardly any poetry about sport and even less music. Except for the songs of Max Boyce about rugby, I can't think of any original music at all, although I believe that a Dutchman wrote a symphony in the thirties based on a rugby match at Twickenham. It's true there are rugby songs, but these are rarely about rugby, except for a few such as *If I was a Marrying Type* with its rundown of the sexual connotations of each playing position on the field. Otherwise the so-called rugby songs are largely about loins. In any case, the tunes are not original.

Cricket is the only sport to attract anything that could be called poetry at all, and there is some very good cricket verse. Most people are familiar with Francis Thompson's famous poem *At Lord's* and the verse:

> For the field is full of shades as I near the shadowy coast
> And a ghostly batsman plays to the bowling of a ghost,
> And I look through my tears on a soundless-clapping host
> As the run-stealers flicker to and fro,
> To and fro:
> O my Hornby and my Barlow long ago!

Although my own favourite is a verse by D.L. Jephson:

> Give me a bat full of white grain,
> In the heart of a willow grown,
> With never a peg and never a band,
> I'll force the ball to the outfield land
> With the softened sound of a silken hand
> Smoothing a velvet gown.

In an effort to remedy the sad lack of sporting poetry the *Sunday Times* ran a contest to find the best sporting ballad. As part of the campaign I was requested to write my Saturday rugby round-up in verse. This was not easy since the column usually consists of searing pieces of information like this:

Gloucester notched their third victory in succession when they defeated Bristol by 6–0 at Kingsholm but the game was spoiled when five Bristol men were sent off for arguing with the referee.

Hardly the raw material of epic verse.

In the end I succeeded in producing what was probably the world's first sporting column written entirely in rhyme, and it could well have taken ten years off my life. I shall not bore readers with it all, but sufficient to say it began with the fascinating couplet:

> Oh spare a sad thought for the Saracens then
> Beaten forty to four by the bold Leicester men.

And even that had taken me two hours.

I don't know whether it was the effect of my efforts, but quite honestly I considered many of the winning ballads complete rubbish, full of rumpty-tums and exaggerated sentiments, and incredibly dull in context and verse-form.

The man who really should have written about sport, of course, was William McGonegall, self-styled poet and tragedian, whose appalling verse has been famous for nearly a century. As a poet McGonegall was surely the Coarse Bard of all time, poetry's equivalent of the Extra B full-back as it were, and I feel that he would have been the only person to have done justice to rugby in verse. But as he never wrote any sporting material (unless one counts his Ode on the Death of Prince Leopold) may I be permitted to fill the deficiency with a McGonegall style ode of my own on the subject of the England-Wales match in 1978, when Gareth Edwards got his fiftieth cap?

And oh, everyone at Twickenham did make great glee
For today was the day on which Gareth Edwards they had come to see,
As it was the occasion of the fiftieth time he had played in the Welsh national side, which
Will cause his name in the Hall of Fame forever to have a small niche.

They say the crowd numbered 75 641
Which is more than reckoned by some.

And the game was a positive holocaust
As bad as Waterloo or even worse.

And oh, loud was the Welsh roar as Edwards ran on gladly
But the cheers soon changed to moaning sadly
For Alistair Hignell kicked a penalty or two
And he is captain of Cambridge and weighs fourteen stone two.

Thus at half-time Wales were 6–3 down to be seen
Two penalties to one I wean.
And the Welsh forwards did make much moan
At the manner Horton and Burton caused them to groan.

But oh, things were different in the second half
For Wales had the wind which did make them laugh.
And noble Phil Bennett, with the best intention
Kicked two penalty goals in succession.

And England declared it was a bit thick on them
To be beaten 9–6 by Wales at Twickenham.
But to Gareth Edwards the glory belonged and he
Showed that at the age of thirty-two he has not lost any of his natural
capability.

The match was organized with customary efficiency
By the Rugby Union and their committee
To whom be all thanks and jubilation
And they warned everyone that tickets for the next
International must be applied for without hesitation.

25 The Day Their Dreams Came True

Most of us dream of winning the football pools, of the magic moment when a huge cheque is placed in the hand and all life's worries will be over. Such a dream is especially poignant for a Coarse Sportsman, whose usual fantasy is that now he will be able to *buy* the success which has eluded him on the field. He dreams of the day he will buy up the tennis club and threaten to build on it unless they let him join; of hiring Arnold Palmer to give him golf lessons at 100 dollars a minute; of donating a new stand at Twickenham and having it named after himself. But few people have actually seen that miraculous cheque presented, a ceremony which in this materialistic age must surely be the equivalent of the mystic rites of old, the crowning of the Inca King or the initiation of the Druid priestesses perhaps. The *Sunday Times* sent me along to pierce the veil of the sacred ritual, and here's what happened.

The Voltaire Suite of London's Grosvenor House Hotel might have been ready for a wedding reception, what with the flowers, the canapes and the table full of free booze. It was in fact, set up for something rather different – pay-out day for the lucky winners of half a million pounds on last weekend's Littlewoods football pools.

A small stage at one end of the room was suitably decorated with huge pictures of the two winners, one blacked out as the winner wanted to be anonymous. Flowers (real) and grass (artificial) covered the stage and the organizers had thoughtfully provided two live lambs who added colour by bleating piteously throughout the whole affair. No one quite knew what they symbolized.

The Gentlemen of the Press were commendably early, as they usually are when free food and drink are involved, and there were about fifty people present when a representative of Littlewoods mounted the stage and introduced a Sunderland woman who had won £253 319. Unfortunately, she wanted to remain anonymous, so she was represented by a mysterious masked female, hired for the day, who slunk on to the stage in complete silence, and slunk off again. Then she removed her mask and started to eat sausage-rolls.

Then came the other winner, in person this time, Mr Peter Mason, a thirty-eight-year-old hosiery worker from Derbyshire, and his mother-in-law, who as joint provider of the 30p stake was going to have half the money. Both dutifully bared their teeth for the photographers as comedian Max Bygraves presented the jumbo-sized cheque for £251 952. Smoothly and professionally, with the assured air of one who has himself turned up a winning line on the Great Treble Chance of Life, Max Bygraves took charge, fired off a joke or two ('Blimey, I'd have to work all week to earn this cheque....'), stage-managed five minutes of solid teeth-baring for the cameras, and then rapidly disappeared.

Mr Mason, his wife and his mother-in-law were placed at the disposal of the press. Littlewoods had already thoughtfully handed round their views on life ('I think Peter is the most amiable man on earth ... it must be unique for a mother-in-law to have this kind of relationship with her daughter's husband ... we are a very happy family'). But reporters wanted something more newsworthy.

Unfortunately the Masons were too normal, too nice, and above all too dazed to provide anything really juicy.

'What do you *really* think of your mother-in-law?' a reporter asked Mr Mason amidst a growing din. Mr Mason tactfully parried with, 'What do you think of *your* mother-in-law?'

'Bloody wonderful,' came the reply. 'She's been dead for five years.'

More journalists pressed Mr Mason to reveal the secrets of his winning system, which is based on choosing matches by the dates of various family festivals.

'I put down an 11', said Mr Mason, 'because that's my

daughter's age. And a 21 because she was born on the twenty-first. And then 34 because that's my wife's age, but don't print that. And finally, and this is the important bit, I turn the coupon upside down and start from the bottom.'

At least it sounded like that.

Mr Mason sensibly declined to be drawn, despite the pressure, and every time he stepped out of line added rather optimistically, 'Please don't print that.'

His mother-in-law was equally cagey and frustrated journalists became more and more leading in their questions.

'I expect you were utterly shocked and astounded when you heard the news, Mrs Flint?'

'No, I can't say I was.'

'But surely you must have been completely flabbergasted and dumbfounded?'

'No.'

'Not even petrified, shocked, struck all of a heap?'

'Well if you say so. . . .'

Slowly the throng subsided, the crush eased. Baffled, the reporters dribbled away. The Mason's two children began to look impatient and the boy started tugging at his parents' clothes. Looking highly unflabbergasted, unpetrified and undumbfounded the winners stood discussing what to do after lunch. The two lambs escaped from their attendants and tried to eat the artificial grass. On being defeated they started to nibble the geraniums.

Later Mr and Mrs Mason and Mrs Flint went forth into Park Lane, the richer by a quarter of a million pounds. And nobody knew who they were.

26 *The Buy, Buy Blues*

Every year I swear I'll never go to the Boat Show again, but every January finds me marching into Earls Court like an alcoholic homing on a public bar. The fact is, all yachtsmen are compulsive spenders. They're like kids in a toyshop. That's what they like about sailing, snooping around buying all sorts of gadgets. It's much more fun than heaving on the ocean. After twenty years' sailing you'd think that by now I would have everything I needed, but I still can't pass a chandler's shop without buying something, even if it's only a spare shackle pin to add to the other 150 spares we've got rattling around in the bilge, where they will remain for ever, since we can't get at them.

Mind you, shackle pins are small fry compared with some of the stuff I've purchased. My pride and joy was a spirit cooker made in Korea which rejoiced in the extraordinary name of *The Glow-Fart*. A subsidiary title said it was 'the yachting-man's fiend'. We didn't need it, so I promptly bought it, and it distinguished itself by exploding the first time we tried to light it. My friend Askew suggested we should write to the makers in Korea but we decided that with their obviously limited command of English that would only cause more trouble ('deeply regret explosion of honourable Glow-Fart').

Another of my great purchases was an underwater compass which you strapped to your wrist when skin-diving. Actually, I'd thought it was a watch. I used to wear it like a watch all the time, only it had a basic fault as it's the only compass I know which always points due west. Perhaps it only works under water.

As far as I'm concerned we don't need to employ salesmen at the Boat Show. It's something to *stop* me spending I need. In fact salesmen put me off with their careful reservations about the boat, things like, 'To be absolutely frank sir, the quarter berth is just a trifle restricted in length. Of course, sir, it does mean the bunk is especially suitable for limbless persons, if you should have a crippled relative or friend.'

Incidentally, it's strange that there is no other sport, except golf, where the spending compulsion is so strong as in sailing. It's lucky they don't have a golfing equivalent of the Boat Show or I'd be in there too, desperately buying success, purchasing balls with my initials on, medicated socks, and probably some new device such as an armpit-shaver ('Very few people understand, sir, that long hair under the armpits affects the downswing and can subtract ten yards from the average drive . . .'). Yes, I'd buy an armpit-shaver if there was one in the vain hope it might help, just as I'd buy a wind-vane to stick on top of my trolley, if they made one.

Nobody sneers at you in either golf or sailing for wasting money on expensive rubbish, yet in other sports such as rugby and cricket there's almost a tradition of making do and sticking to old gear, favourite bats, well-loved boots. To quote Tony O'Reilly again, the Lions winger claims that before an England–Ireland international at Twickenham his faithful old boot-laces broke. None of the Irish could help so he tried to borrow a pair from the England dressing-room, where he walked in just as the English skipper was giving his last-minute harangue: 'Don't be afraid of these bloody Irish, lads, they can't do anything right . . . .'

'Very fine indeed,' says O'Reilly, 'And now could anyone lend me a pair of laces for me boots?'

It is noticeable that golf salesmen and sailing salesmen are very much alike. Both speak in hushed, reverent tones as if in the presence of Death (which they might well be if the buyer knew how much it was all going to cost in the end). They quietly and deferentially put forward the claim of the product with an air of, 'It doesn't matter to us, sir, but of course if you prefer not to be up to date. . . .' I have never forgiven the man who sold me a kit for finding top dead centre on my golf balls, the idea being that all balls were not quite round, so you found the top dead centre by floating the ball in a special solution, marked it, and placed the mark upwards whenever you putted. I've forgotten the price of the outfit but it was astronomical, and when opened it consisted of a felt pen, a packet of salt and some instructions.

But to return to sailing. Beware of the brochures describing the new yachts. Have you ever paused to consider why the model girls who advertise yachts are always so thin? (One day there will be a tragedy when one of them slips through her life-jacket.) It's because *thin girls make the boat look bigger*. You couldn't get more than a couple of big-chested, strapping wenches in the well of the average nineteen-footer along with the helmsman, and even then he'd find the view forward like looking at the sea through the Mountains of Mourne. But you can cram any number of those twig-like creatures in and the simple purchaser looks only at the number of faces leering from the cockpit and thinks what a big boat this is.

It is very difficult for the would-be buyer to find out the sailing qualities of his new boat. As far as the brochure is concerned, of course, it sails magnificently (despite the fact that it is so comfortable inside). After all, it's rather difficult to tell in Earl's Court how your yacht will behave in a gale off Cherbourg. A 'test' sail round the harbour doesn't really tell much more. One suspects that despite all the big talk the buyers indulge in about the technical qualities of their purchase, such as sail aspect ratios and the length of the luff, many new boats are bought for their domestic virtues rather than anything else. I know someone who bought a boat chiefly because it had such a good lavatory, a huge pink affair the size of a bathroom, and incorporating a shower. It was such a relief after the bucket they'd been forced to use on their previous boat.

Unfortunately, the yacht was otherwise a disaster. It sailed with all the speed and panache of a very fat old age pensioner shopping at Sainsbury's on Saturday morning. When the engine was started exhaust fumes filled the entire boat. The only thing that worked properly was the lavatory, which was just as well, as they were often at sea a long time thanks to the

Thin girls make the boat look bigger

poor sailing and the erratic engine. As the owner once said, savagely glancing at the toilet as they drifted on to a reef, 'This boat is good for only one thing, and I could do that ashore just as well.'

27 *Sponsored Nightmare*

If the seventies are remembered for anything in sport, it ought to be sponsorship. From their modest beginnings in the sixties, the sponsors moved in until anything that could remotely be considered a sport, from hang-gliding to sheepdog trials, was taken over. Even that stronghold of amateurism, rugby union, succumbed to the lure of money-bags, and to the astonishment of the die-hards, rugby grounds were soon infested by pretty girls giving away free cigarettes. Along with the sponsorship have gone new cup and league competitions and increasing pressure on the players, which has resulted in some opting out through sheer exhaustion. When shall we reach saturation point? Here's a Rugby Round-Up of 1984.

It was an action-packed day for rugby union fans yesterday as the season reached its climax. There were no fewer than thirteen cup competitions on the go, plus several vital League championship and relegation fixtures. But is there too much rugby this time of the year? Typical of the plight of many first-class clubs is that of Coventry, who after a series of drawn cup-ties, have now been playing every day for three weeks.

So far they have won the Turf Cigarette Vase, the Bonio Shield, the Kleenex Cup, the Kellogg Bowl and the Senior Service Plate, having been knocked out of the Kitty Kat Plinth, the BSA Bust, and the Crosse & Blackwell Salver. But the strain of constant competitive rugby has begun to tell, and yesterday, in the fourth round of the Weetabix Shield they were defeated by Gamages, 147 points to 3.

Many Coventry players were completely exhausted before

the match began and two of them had to be tied to the goal posts to keep on their feet. Three more tried to escape by running into the Coundon Road but were dragged back by club officials.

'I don't know how we shall manage tomorrow,' said a Coventry committee-member. 'We've got the final of the Cherry Blossom Plate against Moseley.'

Quins were another first-class club to make a sudden and unexpected exit from the Weetabix competition. They lost away to Upper Basingstoke Vipers by 3 points to nil. Bad luck hit the Quins before the match when their entire front row ruptured themselves pushing the coach out of the mud in front of the changing-shed.

During the game they lost another player who was gored by a bull while retrieving the ball from a field. Even so, Quins still had a chance until their full back collided with a stray sheep and had to be carried off.

'As long as we can keep on getting drawn at home, we have a good chance of a long Cup run,' said the Vipers' secretary.

But the biggest match of the day was at Gloucester, where the home side's 10–nil win over Broughton Park means that they cannot be overtaken as leaders of the RU First Division, and must therefore be winners of the Saniflush Bowl, the third time they have won the magnificent lavatory-shaped trophy since its presentation when the RU accepted the principle of sponsorship.

However, the match may have repercussions. I gather protests may be made about the fact that the sponsors insisted on both touch-judges being dressed as lavatory brushes. In addition the referee wore a jersey with a luminous sign saying, 'I use Saniflush,' which lit up every time he blew his whistle. Before the match and at half-time, the famous Saniflush Beauty Girls paraded round the ground watched by a crowd of 50 000 to whom they threw free toilet rolls (most of which were returned during play).

Altogether, yesterday's League games produced only four draws so RU pools winners can look forward to a big dividend.

Finally, I have received an SOS from Old Millhillians, a

club older readers may still remember. When league rugby first began to spread they decided to opt out and to play only the old-style friendly games. Unfortunately they have now run out of opponents and after playing Old Paulines seventeen times this season (winning nine and drawing one) they asked me to appeal for further opposition. I willingly pass on the appeal. After all, every sport needs its eccentrics and rugby is no exception.

28 The Coarse Acting Show

I always feel amateur drama is one of the most universal of Coarse Sports and Pastimes. Many of us have rhubarbed our way on-stage with a wooden spear (probably in the wrong army). Even those who haven't participated have watched, and observed with horror the sagging scenery threatening to bury the unfortunate cast (a fate most of them would welcome, since they have forgotten the lines). There is in amateur acting that great gulf between the theoretical way of doing a thing and the way in which it actually gets done that is the classic hallmark of a Coarse Sport. In *The Art of Coarse Acting* I define a Coarse Actor (or Actress) as one who can remember the lines but not the order in which they come, but since then I've received a shoal of bitter advice from actors, actresses and angry directors suggesting other definitions, all based on their latest horror-experience. These have included:

One who knows everyone else's lines but not their own.

One who knows when to come on-stage but not where

One who addresses the scenery instead of the audience.

One who remembers the last play better than the one they're actually in.

These suggest new definitions of other sports. Perhaps one might define a Coarse Rugby player as one who knows when to pass the ball but not where; or a Coarse Golfer as one who addresses the turf instead of the ball. However, acting is unique because it is the only Coarse Sport to become an art-form in its own right. Let me explain. The Coarse element usually occurs accidentally. A rugby player doesn't *deliberately* collapse after running twenty yards, it's just that he's too old to be playing, or he's not fit enough, or he drank and smoked too much in the pub before the game. Nor does a Coarse Actor forget his lines deliberately, it's just that he's written them inside his hat and omitted to bring it on stage. But in recent years there has grown up a fashion for competitive Coarse Acting in which teams from different societies vie with each in macabre displays of theatrical mayhem and ingenious incompetence.

It began with a contest at the Questors, Ealing, as a fund-raising stunt. Among the entrants was a team from the Royal Shakespeare Company, who performed the death of Julius Caesar as it might have been done by the Dunlop Amateur Drama Club (their description). The climax came when Caesar, with six knives sticking out of him, was pursued round the auditorium by Brutus, and escaped through the emergency exit with a last cry of, '*Et tu, Brute.*' Another group finished their performance with the whole cast plastered round the walls supporting the tottering set.

The idea spread and there were other competitions. An outstanding one was at Salisbury Playhouse. It included a whodunnit by a National Theatre team, which had a butler who aged every time he entered the room, so he started off about twenty-six and finished up around eighty. There was another murder mystery in which the killer's gun refused to fire and he handed his victim a glass of whisky with the words, 'Drink this – it's poisoned.' There was also a remarkable version of *Moby Dick* with a cardboard whale, manned by six actors, which broke in half. Both parts careered blindly about the stage, trying to get together.

The apogee of the Coarse Theatre movement came in 1977 when a group of us took a specially-written production to the Edinburgh Festival under the title of *The Coarse Acting Show* (since published by Samuel French). One can only describe it as the theatrical equivalent of holding a cricket match in which everyone has one arm tied behind their backs. Still the audience liked it, which proves what I've suspected for a long time, that people can become tired of success and like to see failure given a chance for a change.

Yet, as always, the made-up version pales into insignificance before real life. It was only a few weeks after the first Coarse Acting competition that I found myself in an experience so bizarre that it made its carefully constructed deliberate disasters look prosaic by comparison. It all began when I slipped during a performance of *Treasure Island*, breaking my leg and dislocating my elbow. It was a special performance for old age pensioners and as I lay groaning while an ambulance was sent for, they discussed my case knowledgeably. It was obviously far more entertaining than the play. I distinctly heard a woman in the front row of the stalls say, 'I think he's going. My husband turned that colour just before he went.'

The really grotesque element came later when I was carried into the casualty ward of the local hospital. My arrival caused some alarm. To start with, I was dressed in eighteenth-century seaman's costume, with a two-foot-long beard stuck to my chin. One eye was hidden by a patch. A parrot was sewn on one shoulder. One arm terminated in a steel hook. My left leg was strapped up and a wooden leg was attached to the knee. To crown it all a long dagger was sticking from my chest, which was covered in artificial blood.

The nurse, hardened though she was, blenched at the sight and seemed undecided which deformity to treat first. My real injuries were hardly to be noticed, compared with the stage ones. She decided to start with the knife which was firmly stuck in a block of wood strapped to my chest. She pulled and nothing happened. She pulled again. Eventually in desperation she knelt on my chest and tugged as hard as she could; this time the knife came out complete with block of wood. At that point she decided to go for the doctor.

The doctor arrived, all bustle and efficiency, and disguised his surprise at the apparition on the bed with an effort.

'And what seems to be the trouble?' he said with masterly understatement.

'It's my arm and leg,' I explained, pawing the air feebly with my hook.

He looked at the hook, the parrot, and the wooden leg, and then he turned to the nurse and said, 'They really shouldn't

'And what seems to be the trouble?'

send these orthopaedic cases here. I'll make an appointment for him to have a proper limb fitted tomorrow.'

It was midnight before they finally finished with me. I persuaded them to treat my dislocation and the broken leg eventually, but they became very suspicious when they took off my coat and found that the parrot and steel hook were both an integral part of it.

The last words I remember hearing as they gave me the anaesthetic were, 'I'm not sure if there isn't some suspicion of mental trouble, here, nurse.'

A 'suspicion of mental trouble'. Yes, I think that sums up Coarse Acting.

29 *Things that will Never Change in Sport*

To mark the Queen's Silver Jubilee in the sporting field, the *Sunday Times* asked me to project myself back to the start of Her Majesty's reign in 1952 and forecast the next twenty-five years from the point of view of a quarter of a century ago. The following masterly survey resulted.

This first weekend of June 1952, as preparations for next year's Coronation go busily ahead, let's look forward to what sport can expect in the next decade or so of the new Elizabethan era ushered in by our radiant young Queen.

First, let's hope that England at last escapes from the dismal series of humiliations undergone by our cricketers, footballers and athletes since the war. I firmly believe that meat rationing is to blame for this. Our cricketers, on last year's tour of Australia by F. R. Brown's side, were astonished to see Australians tucking into breakfasts of chops and steaks, and eating in one meal a whole English family's meat ration for a week – and no wonder when it is a miserable 1s. 2d. worth a head. You just cannot build fast bowlers on Woolton Pie and Victory Stew.

Many blame the failure of the British forwards last winter against the Springboks on the same cause. Something must have been responsible for the South African's sweeping success, with thirty wins out of thirty-one matches.

I fear we can hope for little comfort in the Helsinki Olympics in July, where the great Czech, Emil Zatopek, must surely be competing for the last time. Perhaps at last the four-minute mile barrier will be cracked, but I doubt it. The human frame was just not designed to run that fast. One thing is certain. If the magic figure is achieved, it won't be an Englishman who'll do it.

But let's look on the bright side. England cricket certainly has a promising hope in the young Yorkshire fast bowler, Trueman, F. S., who bowled so well against the Indians at Leeds. If he can curb his fiery temperament, this lad could go far.

The success of Dollery, H. E., in leading Warwickshire to victory in the County Championship last year, has now been followed by the appointment of another professional in Hutton, L., to lead England in the current series against India. Never have the opportunities been better for professional cricketers than today. Many of them can now afford motorcycles, and some even have cars. The days when a professional cricketer took off his bicycle clips before batting are over.

Thank heavens our cricketers have more sense than certain tennis players who have joined up with Jack Kramer's appropriately named professional 'circus', which will doubtless fizzle out when the novelty wears off. Moreover, they will certainly not follow the example of footballers and make outrageous demands. The latest move of the Football Players' Union, under its chairman, Jimmy ('soccer slaves') Guthrie, is to try and insist on a closed shop for footballers. One wonders exactly how much farther footballer's demands will go. They already have a maximum wage of £14 a week and a minimum of £7, with respectively £7 and £5 a week in the close season plus such perks as a house and ration-free meals. I was told the other day of a Second Division player who habitually arrives at the ground in a taxi!

With transfer fees up to a record £35 000, the game just can't afford wages like this, let alone to increase them. Many clubs are already struggling, and I would not be surprised if that famous old team, Accrington Stanley, did not eventually have to shut up shop.

It is outside our traditional fields of football and cricket that this country must look for its successes, and at least we can hold our heads high in golf, with Max Faulkner as the reigning Open champion. No doubt he will be one of a string of similar

British champions over the next twenty years.

A sport in which we lead the world is motor-cycling, where Geoff Duke has once again swept the board on a Norton. Fashions in sport may come and go, but no country will ever supplant Britain's motor-cycle dominance, founded as it is on a basis of the world's strongest motor-cycle industry.

What of the future? The outlook is as uncertain as the international situation. It is difficult to be optimistic, with the war in Korea dragging on and National Service playing havoc with sport by taking away our best young men.

Fortunately our great traditions are in safe hands. Whenever I become depressed about the antics of professional footballers, I think of that greatest of amateur games, rugby union. Here is one game that will never sully itself with commercial interests. The idea of a rugby union club accepting free kit for a publicity stunt is simply too fantastic to be entertained. We shall never see rugby grounds plastered with hideous advertisements, or filled with girls offering free cigarette samples.

Cricket has some of these qualities, too. To me, the enduring respect for tradition which is such a feature of the game is symbolised by Lord's, where I like nothing better than to contemplate a good game, such as Gentlemen *v.* Players, with a pint of beer in my hand from in front of the historic Tavern. Thank heavens MCC are not the sort of brutal philistines who would tear down that lovely old building and replace it with a modern monstrosity. It is about as likely as a Scotsman or a South African captaining England at cricket!

Another thing that fills me with hope is the British public. They remain, as always, the most sporting, decent, well-behaved bunch of people in the world. Go to Manchester United or Chelsea on a Saturday if you want to see the spirit that made this country great. There'll be lots of cheering and groaning, perhaps a few boos, but none of the sickening violence and hysteria that.marks football supporters in such countries as Italy, where, believe it or not, they actually have to be fenced in like animals to prevent them attacking players or throwing missiles.

I always feel that the complete hush which fills Lord's when

Sporting, decent, well-behaved

a bowler runs up, or the silence at Twickenham when a penalty is taken, are things that mark us for what we are. There has only ever been one man sent off at Twickenham in an international and it is unthinkable today that anyone would ever be sent packing in a game between two countries.

But all sports must beware of the new menace of television. Already the number of sets licensed has passed the million mark, and sets are getting larger – the new ones have screens as big as fourteen inches. Soon the whole country will be able to receive the transmissions. The effect on crowd sizes could be dramatic and I would stake my reputation that in ten years' time attendances at cricket Tests or rugby internationals will have fallen so low that you'll be able to get a ticket for the asking.

So much for the new Elizabethan era in sport. Yet will it remain Elizabethan? In these socialistic days, when unskilled workers can earn as much as £8 for a forty-four-hour week, when 'power to the people' is the cry, one wonders how long the Monarchy will survive. Some doubt if Her Majesty's reign will last long enough for a Jubilee, and in June 1977 we may be celebrating instead the inauguration of President Aneurin Bevan with lemonade and buns in the Attlee Memorial Hall.

30 *Fiona's Honeymoon Night*

Fiona telephones:

'Hullo, hullo ... is that you, Penelope? Yes it's *me*, Fiona.
Yes, I *know* it's strange to ring someone up on your honeymoon night, but I've just got to tell you ... Rodney can't do
it! What's that? No, darling, he can do *that* – well, just, at any
rate – but he can't come to the international at Twickers with
you and Jonathan next week. Why not? Darling, he's in jail.
Yes dear, that place where they put your Daddy after he
smashed up the Jag ... no, I'm not trying to drag up old
wounds ... Yes Darling, it must have been positively grotty
in Pentonville ... well you see, it was all the result of the
wedding. Yes, I know you couldn't be there. Yes, dear, we did
thank you for the cake-dish. And everyone else who gave
cake-dishes. It was all Daddy's fault really. He started drinking at dawn. I know he did because he got up early to make
the tea and when I came down an hour later he hadn't even
put the kettle on – he was just sitting by the radiator with a
bottle of champagne. I asked him what he was doing and he
said it was the happiest day of his life. No, dear, it was *not* a
nice thing to say. He didn't mean it as a compliment. Well,
honestly, by the time he came to take me to the church he was
in a terrible state. He couldn't find his top hat anywhere and
we had to go without it. Then he insisted on opening the car
windows and shouting at people in the street. I don't know
what the driver thought, but we got to what Daddy insisted on
calling the "sacred edifice" all right, and Mummy and I got
him inside by holding each arm, and I sort of led him up the

aisle. Then we went through the ceremony and Rodney looked absolutely monumental in his morning-suit and it all went like a bomb until they came to that bit "with my body I thee worship" at which Daddy burst out into peals of drunken laughter and Mummy had to put her hand over his mouth to shut him up. The vicar looked outraged, especially as he hates Daddy ever since he took change for ten bob from the collecting plate. Then he loudly asked if there was any just cause or impediment and so forth, and of course there was complete silence, and in the middle of it all a Welsh voice muttered quite distinctly, "I should think there was," and I realised that awful creature Taffy Owen had got into church. He was sitting with the rest of the fourth XV at the back. Anyway, to cut a long story short, we got through it all (although I didn't like the way Rodney hesitated on, "I do") and we marched out down the aisle and when we got outside there were the players with an arch of corner flags. It was wonderful. And then to my horror as we were marching under this arch I saw Taffy holding one of the flags and as we passed he said quite distinctly, "I've had her. And I didn't enjoy it." Honestly, I nearly *died*. And Rodney must have heard, because he got all sort of tensed up and he's always been jealous of Taffy but that's old history now. Well, anyway, off we went to the reception and Daddy was *beastly*, he kept slapping Rodney on the back and shouting, "Better you than me, old son," and pouring brandy into his champagne, and then he went over and actually shook Taffy by the hand, although he hadn't even been invited. I thought I was going to *howl*. Well, eventually we got to the speeches, and it was obvious by then that Rodney had been affected by Daddy's champagne and brandy because instead of saying a few words he went on and on and on. And then he started to become absolutely revolting and began making alleged humorous remarks like, "As a good forward I shall certainly push hard tonight," and then he told the most obscene story I have ever heard in all my life and Mummy's relatives' faces were going blacker and blacker and I just sat there *frozen* with horror. I was sure Uncle George was going to make a scene. Mercifully Rodney forgot the end of his story and Tubby Chapman, the best man, leapt up and thanked him and said he might be a joke as a full back but he was sure he would find touch tonight, and they all howled with mirth and Daddy fell off his chair. Eventually Mummy and I had literally to drag Rodney away so we could change, and we were going to be driven in Tubby's car only when we got outside, it had been jacked up and all four wheels removed. So we went in Daddy's car (thank heavens Daddy refused to drive and Tubby did instead) and came back in Rodney's to say goodbye. Well, believe it or not it took another hour and a half to get Rodney away and a lot of it was Daddy's fault, he kept getting them together in a scrum and heeling someone's top hat. Eh? No, I don't know whose hat it was ... Taffy's, I hope ... but eventually we got away and drove off to the secret honeymoon hotel ... no, dear, nowhere very exciting, Henley-on-Thames if you must know. Rodney had originally booked us in at Maidenhead but I made him change it. Well there *is* a limit.... Anyway, on the way, the most cataclysmic event occurred. A policeman stopped us on the Motorway and asked Rodney if he was aware that he had *a stair-carpet trailing from the back of the car*. They must have tied it on while we were waving goodbye. Well, to cut a long story short, the policeman got a sniff of Rodney's breath (not that that was difficult, you could have smelt the brandy five hundred yards away) and asked him to breathe into a bag and Rodney hiccupped and said he had a right to trail a stair-carpet if he wanted, and the policeman said, "Not when it's got Star and Garter Hotel printed all over it," and then Rodney was rude to the policeman and the next thing I remember was sitting in the police station while they locked Rodney in some dungeon or other, and told me he'd come before the magistrate in the morning. So here's little Fionakins sitting in the bridal suite at Henley-on-Thames on her ownsome and all her friends imagining her revelling in an orgy of positive lust. No, dear, I don't intend to come back to London tonight. Can you imagine what Daddy would say if his own daughter rang the front doorbell on her honeymoon night? Besides, I've got to attend the trial or what ever they call it, tomorrow ... and to think I voted for the return of flogging at the Young Conservatives ...'